SUPPORT FOR WOMEN WHO ARE AFFECTED
BY THE TRAUMAS OF LIFE

*Un*Hooked!
7 Steps To
Emotional Freedom

Life changing steps to unhook from your past

Karen Wells, M.Div.

ISBN-13: 978-1466320789

"The LORD is close to the brokenhearted
and saves those who are crushed in spirit."
Psalm 34:18

I dedicate this book to all the women who have allowed me to walk alongside them on their journeys of healing.

Acknowledgements

I want to thank God for touching me with His love, empathy, and desire to listen to hurting women. Without His grace, I do not know where I would be in my own life today. God has opened the door for me to live my best life possible and now I have the privilege to share my journey of hope with other women. I pray every woman knows that she can seek her best life possible in Him.

I want to thank my husband, Simon, for being willing to edit, read, and listen to me throughout this book project. He is my best friend and support.

I want to thank all those who have given me feedback on this 7-step process. It has been very valuable and encouraging.

I want to thank my graphic designer Christine Dupre, my editor Susan Lawrence, and my transcriptionist Alma Noefe. Thanks for all your help.

Karen

Table of Contents

Introduction

Congratulations for deciding to unhook! I am confident that as you put into practice the principles laid out in this book, you will find freedom from the hold that past painful experiences have on you. You *can* own your life instead of letting your life own you. If you have experienced a painful past and find that you live in that "past" more than you live in the "here and now," this book is for you.

When I look for a book that offers support to develop in personal growth, I tend to wonder how the author determines that what they have to say will benefit me. Perhaps a similar question has crossed your mind also, so I'd like to share a bit of the story behind why I felt led by God to write this book.

It probably makes sense that my career choice as a mental health therapist has played a big part in me even being able to write on this subject. There is no doubt that the thousands of hours I have sat with hurting and broken-hearted women gives me a deeper understanding of the painful journey some women walk in their effort to gain freedom from a story that has held them hostage far too long.

The seven steps I outline in this book have been primarily formulated due to the similarities of emotional and spiritual struggles I find a majority of the women I work with seem to gravitate to. Regardless of their actual story, the healing needs for most women seem to be consistent across the board. I began teaching workshops on these seven steps so women could process through their healing on their own, instead of only having to go to a counsellor for support. I have since decided to present the self-help process in a book, so more women can access this material.

Yet this is not the only reason I decided to write this book. I myself have walked through the *Unhooked!* process. I've lived and worked through all seven steps, and I know they really work. I feel if these steps have helped me, then there are other women who can also be helped by what God has shown me in regards to healing from past pain.

Let me be the first to say that I do not suggest I have a handle on all of *your* specific needs though. I only know what I have experienced, and have seen other women come through. Yet I have a sense that yours looks pretty similar. So, even as you make the decision to grapple with the strategies I have outlined in *UnHooked!*, I know that ultimately the Holy Spirit will be your true Teacher and Healer, just as He is mine.

I've walked with many women who have followed, dug in, and worked hard through these steps, and today they are living changed lives. They are women who came to me with no hope, feeling they could never get unhooked from something that had happened to them. Now, they're experiencing a whole new world of freedom. It is sometimes hard to believe they're the same women!

I'm not promising this healing process will be easy or painless. Actually, in some steps it will feel quite the opposite. After all, you have "hooks" that have been deeply embedded throughout your life. Removing these hooks means ripping through many scabs, and the tearing from these hooks may cause festering for a while.

Don't let that stop you. Go into your healing journey fully aware that you have a job to complete – getting your life back!

Everything I present in this book is founded on my belief that God is the ultimate Healer of our lives. I believe He has provided principles in life that we should follow in order to have the best life possible. Had I not come to know God through Jesus Christ, I know I would not be where I am in my life today. Yes, I might have found some degree of personal healing from my past painful experiences, but not to the degree of wholeness I now live. Because of Christ, I have found a deeper wholeness spiritually, emotionally, mentally, and relationally.

I am reminded of an experience I had early in my Christian life while being a part of a Youth With A Mission drama entitled "Toymaker and Son." At that time in my life, I was still a very emotionally wounded woman and often believed God really did not care for me as He did for others. I so desperately wanted His approval and determined it would be confirmed to me if He allowed me to have a "big" role in the drama. After all, then I would know He saw me fit to be used in an important way for Him.

Yet, as the roles were being doled out to everyone, I felt so desperately unworthy and overlooked. No big role was coming my way. As a matter a fact, they were down to the last two roles and I had not even been called yet! My mind flooded back to my elementary school days when we would be broken into teams during our physical education class. Inevitably, I was the last or second to last person picked for the team. I often heard, "Yeah, okay, I guess we will pick Karen." How horrible it felt to not be truly wanted.

So there I was, silently weeping in my heart that God, too, did not want me. But then something incredible happened. I heard the leader say, "Karen, you will be the china doll." Immediately, I felt the Lord impress on me that He saw me as valuable as china, and that He was taking very good care of me. He cherished me and encouraged me that my worth was far beyond average. How intense I felt His love at that moment. But that was not the end!

In this drama, I was a blind china doll, and the Toymaker's Son (representing Jesus) came to me and gave me sight! Not just physical sight, but spiritual sight. He gave me the ability to see Him for who He is: a kind, loving, and gracious God. Then, as the play continued, the Toymaker's Son took me in his arms and danced with me across the stage. The liberty I experienced to freely be in sync with Jesus was so powerful in this role.

I do not think this story is just for me. I believe that God wants you to know that you too are as a "china doll" to Him.

14

You are of more worth and treasure than you realize. God wants you to see Him for who He is and find freedom to "dance" with Him along your journey of life.

As the blind china doll in the drama, I had to grope across the stage, hoping that someone would see my need and come to my rescue. How I thank God that He came to me while I was groping through my healing of a painful past in my real life! I feel that God has given me some insight into how that journey looked, and I want to share that same path with you. May you come to "see and dance" as I have.

I don't want to assume that every person reading this book has a personal relationship with God. You may not hold any faith at all. This book is still for you. God's principles are sound, regardless of your own faith beliefs. Yet, if you find yourself drawn to wanting to know more about God as you begin your healing journey, be neither afraid nor surprised. You see, without God you might feel you have a good life, but with God you will have the *best* life. So if having the best life is your deepest desire, trust that God knows how to get you there. If somewhere during your journey of healing you recognize that you need Christ, you can go to the *Spiritual Help* (pg. 271) section of this book and learn more about this decision.

My greatest desire is to see women living a life of freedom from the junk of their past. I believe that women who live a life of wholeness – emotionally, mentally, relationally, and spiritually – have the ability to change their world and those around them for Christ. Now that's an unhooked life!

In Him,

Karen

Step 1: Acknowledge Past Experience

Step 2: Recognize And Feel Feelings

Step 3: Name The Loss

Step 4: Understand The Grief Cycle

Step 5: Challenge Your Beliefs

Step 6: Choose To Forgive

Step 7: Let Go And Live In Today

Sandy's Story

Before I started counselling with Karen, my life seemed like it was over. I had no hope of recovery from the sexual abuse that had occurred to me, and my marriage was in shambles.

I thought the only way to find peace was slitting my wrists. Something stopped me. I now know it was God. I realized that I needed to seek help. I visited Karen's website and realized her Unhooked! 7 Steps To Emotional Freedom program to recovery was exactly what I needed.

17

When I had my first meeting with Karen, she told me that God values all of us as a 10/10 and that we need to value ourselves the same. I told her I valued myself as a (minus) -150 out of 10. I was full of guilt and shame. Very slowly, we started working through my stories. The 7 steps made so much sense!

Step 1: Acknowledge Past Experiences

I had pushed them down inside me so they couldn't hurt me. I did not want to go near them.

Step 2: Recognize And Feel Feelings

I only allowed myself two feelings – anger and sadness – but I didn't act on those feelings. Again, they were pushed way down. Plus, I really did not know any other feelings besides those two.

Step 3: Name The Loss

This step was so important to me because once I identified my losses, I could figure out which ones I could gain back. Amazingly, there were many losses I regained, which gave me such strength.

Step 4: Understand The Grief Cycle

I learned to normalize my emotions. It's okay to feel different emotions and realize that they can't hurt me.

Step 5: Challenge Your Beliefs

Once I knew the difference between truth and lies (like the sexual abuse wasn't my fault even though I thought it was for years), it was easier to change my way of thinking.

Step 6: Choose To Forgive

When I first started with Karen and saw that this was a step, I told her, "No way....not going to happen!" In three short months, I have learned to not only forgive, but also to have peace with it. In order to be totally free from it all, I needed to forgive. God forgives me, and this was the one step I had a choice about. I could choose not to forgive and not be totally free OR forgive and be at peace.

Step 7: Let Go And Live In Today

I have let it go. I'm not saying I still don't have bad days, but I'm not suicidal anymore. Karen has taught me strategies on how to deal with thoughts, flashbacks, and memories.

Karen has taught me to give everything to God, the importance of prayer, and most of all, to realize that thoughts cannot hurt me. It's what I do with those thoughts that will determine my future. Identify them, acknowledge them, and then let them go. Live in the present, not in the past.

I cannot change what happened to me, but I can certainly change how it affects me. I have become a much more confident, assertive, and content person since Karen came into my life. I thank her for showing me that I can live a healthy and peaceful life, and if I continue to walk with God, all things are possible.

Sandy

Step 1: Acknowledge Past Experience

Step 2: Recognize And Feel Feelings

Step 3: Name The Loss

Step 4: Understand The Grief Cycle

Step 5: Challenge Your Beliefs

Step 6: Choose To Forgive

Step 7: Let Go And Live In Today

An Overview Of The 7 Steps

You *can* own your life instead of your life owning you, even if you've come from a painful past or experienced a crisis or tragedy. You can learn to live in the "here and now", instead of your "past".

In order to move on, you need to make the decision to unhook yourself from the past negative stories that own how you live today. You might wonder, "How can I acknowledge an experience that happened to me without

21

letting it own or control me?" That's exactly what *Unhooked! 7 Steps To Emotional Freedom* is all about.

We will take the time to explore each of these steps individually as we work through *Unhooked! 7 Steps To Emotional Freedom.* This overview is simply to plant seeds you'll water and nurture later.

The *Unhooked!* steps can change your life so you will experience a new world of freedom. You see, we're all the same in many ways.

 We all have different stories, yet the emotional pain we experience, and the healing needs we have, are similar.

That is why the following seven steps can benefit anyone.

THE 7 STEPS

Step 1: Acknowledge Past Experience

The first step is to acknowledge your past experience. We often do not recognize the impact of our stories because we haven't stepped out of denial, accepted our full stories, and started talking about them.

Step 2: Recognize And Feel Feelings

We need to recognize and feel emotions. We're often afraid of our emotions. We're afraid to let them stay with us. We find unhealthy ways to run from them. Feelings aren't good or bad. They just are. Feelings aren't the issue. The issue is how we deal with feelings.

Step 3: Name The Loss

When we experience something tragic or we've done something we regret, we experience loss. Along with the primary loss of the specific experience or choice, there are many secondary losses we might not be aware of, acknowledge, or take time to figure out. As you explore and define these secondary losses, you'll begin to feel unhooked and start experiencing freedom in your life.

Step 4: Understand The Grief Cycle

Everyone grieves, whether it involves a small loss or a big loss. As you name the loss, you'll become aware of the grief cycle. Women often feel there's something wrong with them or that they're not handling things well. They can feel as if they're going crazy. Often times, they're experiencing common components of grief yet do not realize it. Understanding the grief cycle can help normalize struggles.

Grieving isn't the problem. The problem comes when you get stuck in a particular aspect of the grief cycle. Sometimes you move through the grief cycle quickly, and sometimes you creep through it. As we later explore the specifics of the grief cycle, keep in mind that the pace of moving through grief isn't as important as the process of the actual movement itself. We'll also look at what's normal and what's unhealthy ways of dealing with grief.

Step 5: Challenge Your Beliefs

You have beliefs you've brought from your childhood into your present life, even if you think you haven't or aren't aware of what they are. Your childhood experiences are part of your story. Some beliefs are faulty, including the unhealthy ones that continually pull you back into the past.

You'll learn how to recognize faulty beliefs, so you can challenge lies and then embrace truths. As we dig deeply into Step 5, you'll get specific tools for recognizing truth from lies. The problem is that lies can look truthful, so you can be deceived. The great thing is that Jesus promises in John 8:32, "Then you will know the truth, and the truth will set you free".

Step 6: Choose To Forgive

Forgiveness is very hard for many women, and we'll address various reasons why this is. The forgiveness process is often the area where the most significant changes take place in women's lives. Forgiveness has powerful spiritual and emotional outcomes that can redirect your life.

Step 7: Let Go And Live In Today

The final step in the *Unhooked! 7 Steps To Emotional Freedom* is letting go and living in today, not yesterday or tomorrow. You must learn to recognize when you're slipping back into the past, and find strategies for living in the present. You can look into your past to learn from it, but it is your present that builds the future.

MORE SUPPORT

I've included a prayer at the end of each chapter that I invite you to speak out to God. It is found under the heading *"Prayer"*. It is my firm belief that the surest path to healing involves asking God to be your guide. After all, "If God is for [you], who can be against [you]?" (Romans 8:31).

At the end of each chapter I have also provided you with some reflection questions to pray and ponder over. They are found under the heading *"Digging In"*. Please take the time to work through them. Ask the Holy Spirit to reveal things to you. Write down your answers and begin implementing changes you need to make. This "homework" is the foundation to your forward movement.

If you find that working through these questions seem too intense to do alone, then I encourage you to find someone with whom to talk about them with. Perhaps it will be a friend, pastor, or a counsellor. You can also consider participating in the *Unhooked! 7 Steps To Emotional Freedom* webinar coaching support group I offer. This is not meant to be an intense counselling program but rather a coaching support group. You can learn more at www.unhooked7stepstoemotionalfreeedom.com.

I have also included some scriptures at the end of each chapter for you to claim towards your healing. They are under the title, *"His Words Of Hope"*. God is truly the ultimate Healer and His Word is a comfort you can always depend on.

Prayer

Dear God,

I'm anxious and excited about the journey I have ahead of me. Take my fears and comfort me. Take my excitement and let me grow more bold and hopeful with each new step.

In Jesus' Name,

Amen

Digging In

Although this chapter is an overview of the 7 steps, take the time to jot down any questions that have come up for you. This way, as you go through the steps you will be able to come back to this page to be certain your questions have been answered.

Step 1:

Step 2:

Step 3:

Step 4:

Step 5:

Step 6:

Step 7:

His Words Of Hope

† "Carry each other's burdens, and in this way you will fulfill the law of Christ" (Galatians 6:2).

† "I press on toward the goal to win the prize for which God has called me heavenward in Christ Jesus" (Philippians 3:14).

† "Cast all your anxiety on Him because He cares for you" (I Peter 5:7).

† "Be strong and take heart, all you who hope in the LORD" (Psalm 31:24).

† "Let us not become weary in doing good, for at the proper time we will reap a harvest if we do not give up" (Galatians 6:9).

† "Finally, brothers, whatever is true, whatever is noble, whatever is right, whatever is pure, whatever is lovely, whatever is admirable - if anything is excellent or praiseworthy - think about such things" (Philippians 4:8).

Step 1: Acknowledge Past Experience

Step 2: Recognize And Feel Feelings

Step 3: Name The Loss

Step 4: Understand The Grief Cycle

Step 5: Challenge Your Beliefs

Step 6: Choose To Forgive

Step 7: Let Go And Live In Today

The Biggest Lie Women Believe

The following information I am going to share with you is foundational for you to grasp in your heart and mind. You will find yourself being pulled back into your old patterns of thinking if you do not have a clear understanding of what this biggest lie is. This false belief goes undetected in so many women. The struggle is that this lie is taught to us throughout our lives – without people realizing they are teaching it to us.

This lie has been around for ages. It looks like a reasonable way of thinking, so it is often not questioned. I, myself, never questioned it for years. My parents taught it to me, my education system taught it to me, my employers taught it to me, and even to some degree, some churches have taught it to me.

It has also been taught to you.

So what is this teaching that I am so concerned about? What could be the biggest lie I see being spread? It's really a simple statement, yet very powerful. Here it is:

 The biggest lie that women believe is that their value is *equal* to their life experiences and character.

At first glance you may not understand why this is an untruth. After all, our behaviors, actions, and motives (character) need to be mature. And of course, we tend to believe that a majority of our life experiences (both good and bad) are most often something we deserve, or at least had some input in. "Be a productive member in society," we are told. "Be the missionary, not the mission field."

Don't get me wrong. I am the first to agree that making mature, healthy decisions and actions better our lives and our society. Plus, as Christians our lives are to reflect God's principles in how we live. Yet, if we decide behavior is the criteria for our value, we are in big trouble. That would mean there are levels of value for people. The no-gooder, the abused, the wealthy, and even the average person is only valued by what each contributes to the world or what experiences have happened to them.

So what is so wrong about this belief? Why would I say it is foundationally a lie? Although I do accept that we should strive to have a quality character and that we should strive to desire good life experiences (I call this our "life growth stuff"), I do not agree that this life growth stuff *equals* our value.

The truth is that God does not determine our value by our life growth stuff. God has a different criteria.

 Our value comes from the fact that we are created in the image of God as human beings.

Nothing more, nothing less. We are 10/10 just because we are human beings. This means all human beings have 100% value.

FALSE BELIEF

VALUE   =   CHARACTER

EXPERIENCES

TRUE BELIEF

We are a 10/10.

We are valuable because
we are created in the image of God as
HUMAN BEINGS.

Our character and experiences play a great part
in our
life growth

but are not an indication
of our intrinsic value.

It is so important that you grasp this truth. Without it, you will find yourself struggling to work through the *Unhooked! 7 Steps To Emotional Freedom* steps. This is because your heart and mind will want to find justification for why you do not deserve to be unhooked.

If you believe there are strings attached to your freedom for healing then the "life growth theory" will fit in just fine. Yet if you accept that your value is separate from what "life" has brought you, then you can freely decide that you can heal *in spite of* what you have done or what others have done to you. That means that even a woman who has been sexually or relationally abused, or has even made the tragic decision of abortion is also a 10/10!

Do you see the major difference? Do you see that you cannot earn your value, but that it was already given to you at conception? God created you with value. There's no other reason you need for permission to value yourself.

my life *Every woman I share this information with almost exclusively agrees that human beings are 100 % valuable - except often they do not accept this for themselves. I ask them to think of a child. I ask if that child is 100% valuable. "Absolutely!" they say. I then ask what the common denominator is between them and that child. "That we are both*

35

humans," they respond. I ask why they believe their value has decreased if the criteria is humanness, not life growth stuff. The light bulb goes on and they realize that they have permission from God to believe they are valuable regardless of what has happened in their lives.

This principle is so important to believe. You need to remind yourself of it throughout your journey of healing. You will need to separate truth from lies so you can walk through your past story with confidence that you can love yourself in spite of the past.

By the way, you are a 10/10 whether you feel like it or not.

 Truth is about facts, not feelings.

As you begin to know and accept this truth, your feelings will eventually line up with the truth. Over time you will be able to discern when lies try to persuade you to reject this truth.

If you don't realize that you're 10/10, you won't treat yourself as a 10/10. Plus, you will not assume that anyone else sees you as 10/10. In response, you might sabotage relationships and opportunities, expecting the worst. You may even sabotage your relationship with God, determining that He could not possibly fully accept you.

If you need reminders of your value, you can put notes around your house that say "I am a 10/10." Feed yourself this truth. Speak it out loud several times a day.

I need to clarify something very important about what I am saying. When I am discussing how your intrinsic value at conception differs from your life growth stuff, I am not stating that your intrinsic value *eliminates* your need for a spiritual awakening through a personal relationship with Jesus Christ. We are all born into the world with a sinful nature.

 Intrinsic value does not equal sinlessness.

Although all people are valued at a 10 by God (as He is the one who made us of value), we still all need to have our sins forgiven and experience salvation. The marvelous thing is that God provides the way to the complete "living out" of our value, through His plan of salvation and Lordship of Jesus Christ in our life. I talk more directly about your spiritual need in the *Spiritual Help* chapter.

my life *For many years, I lived by feelings. It was like living on a roller coaster, chasing feelings up and down. I was trying to believe in myself according to what my feelings and experiences dictated to me. I did not know there was any other way to live. Then I learned the truth.*

I put the truth of who I am in the front of my mind and told my feelings to get behind me. Whenever my feelings of self-worth didn't line up to this truth, I determined to give the 10/10 principle precedence, and I am now a free woman. God is the "value-maker". He has shown me time and time again that He loves me just for who I am. Thanks to Jesus, I am now able to live out my value without fear of trying to "do the right thing" so I would be acceptable. Armed with God and these truths, my life has changed forever.

Prayer

Dear God,

Thank you that You created me in Your image and that being a human being of 100% value is Your idea. Thank you that I can think, communicate, create, feel, choose, and love. Give me the guidance and ability I need to live out my value.

In Jesus' name,

Amen.

Digging In

Write out your thoughts about the statement, "Your value DOES NOT equal your life experiences and character (life growth stuff)."

In what ways have you been attempting to earn your value?

Do you think there are strings attached to your permission to be free from past painful experiences? If yes, what are they?

What are some ways that you can remind yourself of the 10/10 principle?

Do you think it is necessary to feel something is true before you can believe it is true? If so, from where did you gain that belief system?

Explain the difference between intrinsic value and the sinful nature. If needed, go the *Spiritual Help* section of this book to understand more.

In your own words, write what you've learned from this chapter.

His Words Of Hope

† "I praise you because I am fearfully and wonderfully made; Your works are wonderful, I know that full well" (Psalm 139:14).

† "So God created man in his own image, in the image of God he created him; male and female he created them" (Genesis 1:27).

† "Then you will know the truth, and the truth will set you free" (John 8:32).

† "But God demonstrates his own love for us in this: While we were still sinners, Christ died for us" (Romans 5:8).

† "For you created my inmost being; you knit me together in my mother's womb. I praise you because I am fearfully and wonderfully made...My frame was not hidden from you...Your eyes saw my unformed body... All the days ordained for me were written in your book before one of them came to be" (Psalm 139:13-16).

Step 1: Acknowledge Past Experience

Step 2: Recognize And Feel Feelings

Step 3: Name The Loss

Step 4: Understand The Grief Cycle

Step 5: Challenge Your Beliefs

Step 6: Choose To Forgive

Step 7: Let Go And Live In Today

Are You Stuck In The Past?

Before we get started with the specifics of each step, let's look at some important indicators of *why* you might be living in the past, as well as *how* you'll know you're living in the past. We've all had things happen that we wish hadn't happened, but they did. You don't need to be imprisoned by them forever. You don't have to live in regret. You might think you're alone and that no one has ever experienced the same thing that you've experienced.

You might think there's something wrong with you because you think you're reacting or responding in a way that's different from how others might react. Ecclesiastes 1:9 says, "What has been will be again, what has been done will be done again; there is nothing new under the sun". This includes how we respond to difficult life experiences.

POSSIBLE INDICATORS OF LIVING IN THE PAST

Living With Fear

One of the first indicators to show that you might be living in the past is if you're living fearfully in your present. You might repeatedly say, "I won't do that" or "I'm not going to try that." You might not take many risks, because something in the past has taught you that risk taking is not worth what you think you could lose as a result.

If you're living fearfully, you might have heard someone say to you, "You have such potential. Why don't you step out?" You reply, "No. I won't do that. I would never consider doing that." You say "no," not because you've thoughtfully considered the pros and cons, but because

44

you're frozen in fear. When taken to an extreme, you live your life in a prison of fear.

 Look fear in the face, because it's not as powerful as you think.

Your fear is often of the unknown. Once you actually step out and experience something, you'll likely find that what you feared doesn't deserve all that power. It's certainly not worth living in a prison for.

Living As A Victim

Another indication you're living in the past is if you're living as a victim. Most women who live like victims don't even realize they are. Often it takes someone else to see it and bring it to their attention.

People who live as victims tend to have an "I can't" perspective of life: "I can't change this." "I can't change that." "I can't cause anybody to do anything different." "I can't do this." "I can't do that."

No matter what your situation is, you always have a choice of what you're going to do and how you're going to respond.

If you're in a victim mode, you likely struggle with being too afraid to assert yourself. You settle on the belief that you can't. Victim-thinking people become whiny and wear other people out emotionally.

You can choose not to be a victim. You can take back your life and learn to become assertive, instead of passive. You can begin today to take ownership for where your life is.

(Need to learn how to become assertive and set boundaries? Check out www.mybestlifepossible.com for webinars and workshops on assertive living).

my life *I remember when someone told me I was living like a victim. At first, it angered me. I thought, "You didn't go through what I went through. You have no idea of the pain I'm in. How can you tell me I'm living like a victim? I was victimized!" But I'm glad the person had the courage to confront me and tell me I was letting victimization define who I was. That's what helped me see I needed to change. It was a relief when I stopped believing the lie that I would always be a victim and finally accepted that I could change my life.*

But that meant I needed to take responsibility for my life. It meant I could no longer blame my past experiences for why I acted the way I did. It meant I had to grow up! It also meant I needed to learn how to set boundaries in my life. It was scary to learn how to set boundaries. It was, as I call it, a knee-knocking experience.

If you're the type of person who doesn't know how to set healthy boundaries, if you're overly passive or aggressive, learning how to take control in healthy ways can be absolutely knee-knocking scary. Yet, I've learned how to do it and so can you. What a difference it has made for me to not live like a victim anymore.

Living With Anger

Another indication that you might be living in the past is if you're a very angry person. There are many angry women in the world. The interesting thing is that many women don't recognize it in themselves. Often they label their aggressive behavior as proof of independence.

Numerous women I've worked with have been sexually abused or have had an abortion and experience strong emotional fallout. They're angry even if they don't recognize it. It's evident in the way they communicate, take control of everything, and need to always be right. They're frequently angry at themselves.

 Instead of letting anger swallow you up, use it to change your situations. You can make anger your ally.

This idea is so opposite of how you might understand anger because you've likely only experienced anger as destructive. Whether you're aware of it or not, your anger is building a wall. As long as it's there, you won't be able to fully accept what you want: love, acceptance, hope, and a healthy future. As you take all that anger energy and use it to make changes, you begin to bring the wall down. (Go to www.mybestlifepossible.com for available webinars and workshops on the topic of anger).

Living With Chronic Worry And Anxiety

If you're a chronic worrier or in chronic anxiety, you might be living in the past. Chronic worry and anxiety are indications you don't feel a sense of ownership in your life. You believe the moment you're currently living in owns you, so you consistently think of the negative things that might happen. You're afraid to make the wrong decision, so you make no decision at all, and your life seems like it is falling apart.

my life *I was a worrywart years ago. If I wasn't worrying about something, I was worried that I wasn't worrying enough. I couldn't imagine living through my day without worrying. I had to learn that worry wasn't adding anything to my life. I had to start taking stock of what thoughts and ideas were consistently overtaking my mind. I had to realize that a majority of my worry was based on fears that never came to pass. Hours a day were spent using up my mental energy. My excessive worrying kept me from enjoying my life.*

Jesus said, "Therefore I tell you, do not worry about your life, what you will eat or drink; or about your body, what you will wear. Is not life more important than food, and the body more important than clothes? Look at the birds of the air; they do not sow or reap or store away in barns, and yet your heavenly Father feeds them. Are you not

49

much more valuable than they? Who of you by worrying can add a single hour to his life? Therefore do not worry about tomorrow, for tomorrow will worry about itself. Each day has enough trouble of its own"' (Matthew 6:25-27, 34).

 Worry has no power to change your life.

When you choose to remain in worry and anxiety, you can get to a point of having various phobias and fears that hold you back from living a full life.

Working in the mental health field, I'm aware of the high number of women on anti-anxiety and anti-depressant medication because they feel they can't cope any other way. If you're one of these women, I encourage you to learn how to work through your anxieties and depression *while* taking medication.

 Medication takes the edge off your symptoms, but it cannot change your beliefs.

The most important thing is to learn how to quiet your thinking so you can better challenge false beliefs. Dealing with chronic worry and anxiety will help you move beyond your past.

(Need to learn more about how to defeat worry? Visit www.mybestlifepossible.com for information on webinars and workshops).

Living With Low Self-Value

Another indication of living in the past is when women struggle with low self-esteem (which can also be identified as self-love or self-value). This comes back to your understanding of where you believe your value comes from. Although I already shared this principle in a previous chapter, it warrants being repeated.

When I ask women how much they love and value themselves on a scale of 1-10 (10 equaling 100%), most do not say 10. Numerous women say 1-5, and many others even give me a minus (-) number.

We are all 10/10 because our value is based on the fact that we are created in the image of God as human beings.

This truth never changes. When we *equal* our value to our life experiences and character (life growth stuff), we often punish ourselves because we see that our life growth stuff is far from perfect.

Our value and life growth stuff are not the same! No matter what you have done, what has happened to you, or what others say and do to you, your value is always a 10.

 Your life growth stuff might need some work, but not your value.

Your value comes from the fact that you are created in the image of God as a human being. Your accomplishments are only life growth experiences, not value-based experiences. Your value will never change, no matter what you do or do not accomplish. This should give you the courage to step out in faith, not fear.

God doesn't look at the outward. He looks at the heart, and He has chosen to value you.

If you want to understand the 10/10 principle more completely sign up for the free *Woman to Woman* Ezine and receive the free audio download entitled, "The Biggest Lie Women Believe." It's packed with information to help you recognize where your value comes from.

my life *At one time I rated myself as a minus in value. Now I can claim in humility, yet absolute confidence, that I'm a 10/10. I thank God for making me valuable. My value has nothing to do with my life experiences, which are messy, or my character, which is flawed. It all has to be with the fact that God made me a valuable human being.*

 It's exciting when you embrace your value at 10.

If you can grasp the truth of your value, your life will change. You can place your head on your pillow at the end of the day and, in spite of anything that happened throughout that day, you'll be able to say, "I love me."

Living As A Control Freak

Another indication someone is living in the past is a need for control. We've probably all been control freaks every now and then, but imagine not being able to yield control in the majority of your life, and feeling out of control anytime something is out of the grasp of your influence.

There's a big difference between having some control in your life *versus* controlling life. Having control in your life means making healthy decisions. You make plans in order to create a sense of stability. That's very different than controlling life, assuming if you don't respond in a particular way, something won't happen the way it should. There's an attitude that things have to be done a certain way. There's no flexibility. Control freaks have to tell others how to do something right, how others are doing it wrong, or how others are not doing it the way that they would.

Being a control freak indicates something in your past has hooked you. Perhaps you somehow lost control when

ARE YOU STUCK IN THE PAST?

you were young or you were in a tragic situation. Now you're afraid to trust the world around you, and you respond with a need for absolute control. It's a terrible way to live. Life is full of constant pressure.

my life *Many years ago I spoke with a counsellor who helped me deal with my control issues. It was as if I was hanging onto the end of the rope over a huge cliff. The counsellor asked, "What would happen if you just let go?" I said, "Are you crazy? I'm not going to let go!" And she said, "Let go." I somehow had the courage to let go and give my life over to God's care, trusting that He would direct my life better than I did. I let go. I didn't die.*

I now have a much better life, because I don't try to control everything, everybody, and every experience in it. I have a sense of direction for my life, but I'm also open to accept someone else's perspective or way of doing something. Plus, I no longer feel a need to take ownership for every outcome. What a relief to only have to be responsible for myself and not everyone and everything around me.

The process of letting go of control isn't easy. It takes a lot of work. Since you can only be responsible for how you react to your world and not control how other people

55

react to their worlds, you have to accept that there are things out of your power and influence.

Living In Denial

Another indication of living in the past is living in denial, which people rarely admit on their own (surprise, surprise). For example, someone might say, "Do you think perhaps what happened to you when you were younger (the abuse) has affected the way you're responding in your relationship with your husband?" You say, "Are you kidding? Of course not! That was a long time ago. That's no big deal. It has nothing to do with now." Or, "Do you think perhaps what happened to you when you were a child or teenager might have contributed to why you're so timid in this area?" "No, no! That's ridiculous. Don't even talk about that."

In general, if you respond in a way that says you don't want to talk about things, if you dismiss what someone else might be saying, or if you're not interested in being confronted, you're possibly living in denial.

Not every woman is going to respond in exactly the same way to tragic experiences or decisions they've made, but everybody is affected by what happens in their lives. If you haven't dealt with your experiences, regardless of the impact they've had, you're likely living in denial.

When negative things attach to you, they affect you. Don't live in denial, setting aside your experiences and pretending they didn't happen. Don't let anything hold you back. Be honest about the impact of your experiences, so you can live the best life possible.

Living With Secrets

Many women live with secrets. Secrets can destroy you or imprison your emotions.

 Secrets make you think you have no hope.

You might feel alone in your experience, but remember the Bible says there's nothing new under the sun. Someone else has been through something similar.

You might wonder if a friend, co-worker, or neighbor has experienced something similar to what you've experienced. It's likely some of them have. The number of women who have experienced childhood sexual abuse is estimated to be one in four by the age of eighteen. That is a lot of women who have been affected. There have been millions of abortions in North America alone, leaving countless women experiencing intense fallout from those abortions. Thousands of women live in abusive relationships and suffer in silence.

You might not recognize women who are struggling with sexual abuse, post-abortion distress or relational abuse. That's not because it isn't happening or hasn't happened to them. It's usually because women aren't talking about their experiences. Women keep secrets because they're often ashamed or scared. They don't know how others will respond.

 Secrets are the enemy's way of holding you back so you think you cannot have the best life possible.

You're not alone. Until secrets are exposed, you won't be able to fully help yourself. Are you stuck today? Trust God to help you get free. Don't let your past own you any longer!

I gave you some examples that might indicate that you are letting your past experiences own how you live in the present. Reflect on these suggestions and ask God to help you address any of these hooks that may be stealing your best life possible now.

Prayer

Dear God,

Help me to see how I am living in the past. I do not want to live like this anymore, yet it is so scary to start the journey of healing. Give me the strength and courage to walk with You and get unstuck.

In Jesus' name,

Amen.

Digging In

What hopes and dreams has fear stolen from you?

What stories do you hold that are founded in fear?

What would happen if you looked fear in the face?

How often do you say, "I can't"?

Has anyone ever told you to stop acting like a victim or martyr? What do you think they are seeing?

Describe what it would feel like to have ownership of your life instead of feeling victimized.

Has anyone ever told you that you are an angry person? Are you seeing what they are seeing?

How often do you speak angry words?

How often do you think angry thoughts?

What does your anger protect you from?

How much time a day do you spend worrying?

How often do you wake up anxious? What are the themes?

List all the things you worry about and determine how many of them have come to pass.

Where do you believe your value comes from?

How often do you look at outward behavior, performance and appearance to determine your value?

In your own words, write what you feel you've learned from this chapter.

His Words Of Hope

✝ "Therefore, if anyone is in Christ, he is a new creation; the old has gone, the new has come!"   (2 Corinthians 5:17).

✝ "A fool gives full vent to his anger, but a wise man keeps himself under control" (Proverbs 29:11).

✝ "But now you must rid yourselves of all such things as these: anger, rage, malice, slander, and filthy language from your lips" (Colossians 3:8).

✝ "So do not fear, for I am with you" (Isaiah 41:10a).

✝ "For God did not give us a spirit of timidity, but a spirit of power, of love and of self-discipline" (2 Timothy 1:7).

✝ "The LORD is with me; I will not be afraid. What can mere mortals do to me?" (Psalm 118:6).

Step 1: Acknowledge Past Experience

Step 2: Recognize And Feel Feelings

Step 3: Name The Loss

Step 4: Understand The Grief Cycle

Step 5: Challenge Your Beliefs

Step 6: Choose To Forgive

Step 7: Let Go And Live In Today

The Hurts Of Your Past

There is no denying that life can be full of painful past experiences. It's important to know what has caused hurt in your past and is now impacting your present. You can take ownership of how you're going to face that pain and become whole again.

Aside from the three areas of traumatic experiences I talk about throughout this book (childhood sexual abuse, after abortion distress, and relational abuse), in this chapter, I will give an overview of some other common hurts that might have you hooked. This is not an in-depth overview, yet this may give some understanding of what type of hurts can have long-lasting effects.

COMMON HURTS OF THE PAST

Emotionally Neglectful Parents

There's a difference between abusive parents and emotionally neglectful parents. Emotionally neglectful parents deny the emotional support all children need. Many parents from older generations held the belief that that if children were clothed, fed, and schooled, the parents were fulfilling their parental roles.

Numerous grown adults admit that their parents never said "I love you," and they might still not say it today. It's a sad, but true, reality for many. If emotional neglect happened in your growing up years, you might be emotionally stunted and find it very difficult to give or receive emotional support as an adult.

Abusive Parents

Abusive parents, on the other hand, are often violent. The abuse may primarily be verbal/emotional abuse, but may also often include physical violence, by inflicting physical pain, using aggressive discipline methods, or having loss of physical constraint when they themselves were angry. Abuse also includes withholding food or withholding proper clothing. If you were abused, you've likely carried the effects of it into your present life.

Absent Parents

Another significant hurt of the past is the absence of a parent (or someone else close) during childhood. Losing a parent to death or other separation situations (like divorce) is a painful experience and, unfortunately, people often don't understand how to help young kids and teenagers through such a significant loss. If you've lost someone close to you when you were young, and no one helped you work through it, or you pushed the emptiness away, you're likely still being affected by that loss today.

Adoption

If you've been adopted, oddly enough, you might feel you were abandoned, wondering why your birth parents chose adoption. Even if you grew up in a very loving adoptive home and believe your adoptive parents were a gift from

God, you might still carry a sense of abandonment into adulthood and your relationships. Once you accept the part of your adoption that involves a loss of your biological parents and relationship with them, you can begin to move into your present life with more freedom.

Abortion

Perhaps you learned your mother intended to abort you but changed her mind. You may have experienced abandonment and self-worth issues from knowing this. Compounded by the fact that people don't readily talk about such issues, you might carry around this weight on your own.

Since the effects of having an abortion can be deep and long-lasting, women may often carry the pain through their lives, which can potentially impact how they parent. If your mother has had an abortion, perhaps she's never realized the post-abortion stress she may be experiencing or how her abortion may be affecting you (perhaps in regards to sibling loss). In general, abortion isn't talked about in church, at family gatherings, or over coffee with your friends, so healing can be stunted.

Alcoholism/Substance Abuse

If you were raised in a family with alcoholism or some other type of substance abuse, you've experienced the devastating impact of alcohol/drugs on people's lives. Many people who grow up in substance-abuse lifestyles repeat the cycles of abuse themselves. The cycles can easily become a part of who you are and how you're living. It's important to identify and break the cycle.

Broken Trust Of Authority Figures

Another area that might go unnoticed and not be readily discussed is when people of influence have caused some type of harm to you when you were younger. For example, perhaps a teacher or someone else of significant influence betrayed or mistreated you, and you kept it as a secret, because there were threats and fears paired with the mistreatment.

Trust issues are one of the most difficult losses to regain because trust needs to be earned back after it is broken. There is no quick fix for this. A cautious heart does not easily risk again.

UNHEALTHY WAYS TO MEET NEEDS

 You have legitimate needs, but sometimes you try to get those needs met in unhealthy ways.

Once you've identified some of the hurts of your past, it's important to look at how you might now be trying to meet your legitimate needs in unhealthy ways. Unhealthy habits do impact your present life. You need to unhook from these unhealthy patterns.

We all need to feel loved, valued, cared for, and purposeful. There's nothing wrong with having these needs. The issue occurs when you try to meet your needs in unhealthy ways because of your emotional pain.

Take a look at the graphic on page 72. This represents two examples of how we deal with emotional pain. Notice the phrase "emotional pain" is the common denominator. However, there's an important difference.

The emotional pain with the circle around it represents how you relate to life when you are "hooked." You go around the pain, believing it's too difficult to face. This can involve ignoring, numbing, or deflecting your pain. It can often be evidenced by substance use, depression, or anger. As a result, you feel there's no beginning or end to the problem.

Sometimes you will nearly touch the pain, then quickly move away. Someone might try to get you to talk about it, but you refuse. Or, you begin to talk about it, but because of the pain, you retreat to your unhealthy circle where you feel more comfortable.

Walking through your pain requires you to become vulnerable. That can feel so scary. Yet, it is in those very moments, where you learn how not to be afraid of your emotions and painful experiences anymore. It is during those moments that you sense God's hope and grace.

THE TRUTH ABOUT EMOTIONAL PAIN

Often we choose to go "around" the pain, believing it is too difficult to face, resulting in our feeling there is no beginning or end to our pain. We use unhealthy coping strategies to stay away from feeling the pain.

* * * * * * * * *

If we are willing to go "through" the pain, we can find a beginning and a hope for some kind of conclusion.

Common Denominator = Emotional Pain

Whether you deal with your emotional pain or not, it does not change the fact that you are *already* in pain. Decide to walk through your pain so you can own your life and not let your life own you!

You will experience your pain whether you avoid it or face it.

The important (and risky) part is getting to a beginning point and walking through the pain. You will survive the process. You will make it through.

my life *I remember having to walk through my pain. I was certain I would "drown" in it. I couldn't imagine going through, and survive touching the pain, but I did. I survived and have become a much healthier woman. For many years, I circled the pain. I went around and around. There was no beginning, no end, and no hope. It's important to get help through emotional pain. Ignoring it won't alleviate it. In fact, you'll invite more emotional pain into your life by using unhealthy ways to deal with it.*

SOME UNHEALTHY COPING STRATEGIES

Defense Mechanisms

We often use defense mechanisms to protect ourselves. Here are some examples of some common defense mechanisms utilized by women.

1. Rationalizing

Rationalization is when a person logically justifies unacceptable or irrational behaviors, motives, or feelings. A woman defends her actions by misguided explanations and reasoning. This can involve making excuses, cheating, and lying as a protection mode from the real issue.

Are you a rationalizer? Rationalizing with a rationalizer feels like banging your head against the wall because the rationalizer is moving in circles, not recognizing or admitting she's trying to protect herself from something.

2. Repression

Another defense mechanism is repression. When you repress things, at some level, you forget them. Some things in life are so traumatic that repression is a way you protect yourself after the initial shock. If you repress things, over time you begin to disassociate the event and eventually become unable to connect the dots of what's happening in your life and why you're acting the way you are. The reason for this is because you've forgotten your story on some level.

Sometimes people who have repressed an event will start remembering tragic and traumatic details as they get older. They might question themselves: "Am I making this up? Did this really happen?" God doesn't want you to dig up anything you can't handle, yet I believe He will bring stories and memories to the surface when you're ready and strong enough to handle it. When this happens it is time to start working on it.

 God can help you get unhooked, reclaim your life, and start living in your present.

3. *Avoidance*

Another defense mechanism is avoidance. Instead of forgetting something that's painful, you know what's painful and do whatever you can to move around it, so you don't have to be reminded and deal with it. You avoid what you think will be too painful.

When you avoid, you miss out on a lot in life, because you're afraid to reach out. You place yourself in a bubble and avoid places, people, and anything that might spur memories of bad experiences. In the process, you miss out on the fulfillment of living in the present.

4. Overcompensation

Another defense mechanism is overcompensation, which often comes from a feeling of having to prove worthiness. Perhaps you overcompensate by giving beyond what is healthy for you.

Most women are natural caregivers, which is wonderful. Yet if you don't recognize the difference between self-care and selfishness (thinking self-care is always being selfish) you might continue to give more and more, overcompensating because you feel it is selfish not to. This results in emotional and mental burnout.

You have the right to self-care, which isn't the same as being self-centered and living as if nothing else and no one else matters. Mental, emotional, spiritual, and physical self-care is important and has to be intentional.

 You're worthy of self-care.

The more you become a well-rounded, healthy person, the more you will be able to give of your life to others without burnout.

Addictions

We also meet needs in unhealthy ways through addictions. An addiction – whether it is alcohol, drugs, food, pornography, shopping, working, or something else – can easily take over your life. You feel you can't live without something. You need it to feel normal. Addictions are sneaky. They don't develop overnight. Instead, they slowly become a familiar way of life until you find you cannot function without them or stop the behavior as you expected you could.

Alcohol is one of the most commonly accessed "numbing" substances. The risk of abuse or dependence on alcohol is very high. Binge drinking is one of the most common examples of unhealthy alcohol use.

Another common addiction for women seems to be shopping. You might feel you need to spend, spend, and spend some more, any time there is a stress. It makes you feel good for the moment. In the end, you have a very high credit card bill and a closet full of clothes you'll never wear again. You might wonder, "What's the matter with me?" The issue is an unhealthy way of coping with needs.

Gambling is a similar form of addictive behavior. You look for the thrill of winning and enjoy the risk taking. "Just one more try" you say, yet the one more never seems to end.

Food addiction can also be a common struggle. Binge eating, emotional eating, or under-eating all have the same motive: the need to protect yourself from some kind of emotional pain.

Promiscuity

Perhaps you've ventured into promiscuity to meet needs. Especially if you've had a traumatic past, you might believe the only way to feel loved is through being sexual. In reality, this brings more pain, regret, and turmoil. There is the risk of STD's, facing an unplanned pregnancy, and emotional scarring. Promiscuity can become an addiction for some women.

Blame Games

Another unhealthy way you might be meeting needs is the blame game. Playing the blame game often involves an unwillingness to take responsibility. If you feel a sense that no one really cares about you and life is painful, you can easily slip into a tendency of blaming everybody.

If you've ever spent time with women playing the blame game, you've experienced a stream of complaints. Everyone else is seen as the problem instead of recognizing how their own behaviors are related to their struggles.

Truth Challenge

Another way you can try to meet needs in an unhealthy way is by challenging truth. You might challenge the truth because you find it difficult to accept there's something wrong with how you're living or what you're doing. People who continually challenge the truth are obstinate and appear to think they know everything. These women tend to appear prideful and unteachable.

my life *There was a time in my life when I had built an emotional brick wall around myself. There was no way you would have been able to tell me anything. I was working hard to deny the truth and prove the truth wrong. I used a number of defense mechanisms and addictive-type behaviors in order to protect myself from emotional pain. I also know I was pretty hardened to others trying to reach out to me.*

I remember when people would share principles from the Bible to me before I became a Christian. I challenged every truth brought to me. I thought there was no way I was going to acknowledge I needed something different from what I was doing. I thank God that others never gave up on me and could recognize what I could not – that I was living a "hooked" life. I can honestly say that I no longer go around my emotional pain. Instead I walk through my pain, as often as I have to, in order to live in freedom.

Cursing God

One more way we meet needs in unhealthy ways is by cursing God. Many people curse God for where their lives are today. They decide God is to blame for everything. "If God was real, He wouldn't let this happen." It's not God who is responsible for evil and harm in the world. It is Satan. Satan wants us to blame God, but God isn't our enemy.

my life *God is real. I'm living proof, and I know hundreds of others who are living proof also. You can trust God to give you His love, joy, and hope. Take the risk to trust and reach out to Jesus Christ. I did, and He did not fail me. I've been a Christian since 1982. I'm thankful God showed me I was unhealthily meeting legitimate needs. I needed to come to Him, look for truth, and unhook myself from my life of past tragedy and trauma. I needed to go through the 7 steps of being unhooked.*

Prayer

Dear God,

I've been hurt a lot in my life and I've been angry about it. Help me to begin letting go of these past hurts. Give me the courage to work through these 7 steps so I can experience the freedom I so desperately want.

In Jesus' name,

Amen.

Digging In

Which hurts mentioned are familiar to your past?

Have you ever reached out to someone to help you walk through these hurts? What was the outcome?

If the experience was negative or unproductive, are you willing to try one more time using the 7 Steps? Why or why not?

Which unhealthy coping mechanisms do you use?

What would be the hardest part for you in order to walk through your emotional pain?

What substances do you use to "numb" or "forget for a while"?

Has anyone ever told you they were concerned about your alcohol consumption? How did you respond?

What painful experience are you going around right now?

Have you ever been involved in sexual activity in order to feel loved? How did it make you feel afterwards?

Has anyone ever told you to start taking responsibility for yourself? Why?

Who do you tend to blame for the majority of your struggles? Why?

In your own words, write what you've learned from this chapter.

His Words Of Hope

† "I have sought the LORD, and he answered me; he delivered me from all my fears" (Psalm 34:4).

† "Come to me, all you who are weary and burdened, and I will give you rest. Take my yoke upon you and learn from me, for I am gentle and humble in heart, and you will find rest for your souls. For my yoke is easy and my burden is light" (Matthew 11:28-30).

† "Be strong and take heart, all you who hope in the LORD" (Psalm 31:24).

† "Why are you downcast, O my soul? Why so disturbed within me? Put your hope in God, for I will yet praise him, my Savior and my God" (Psalm 43:5).

† "May the God of hope fill you with all joy and peace as you trust in him, so that you may overflow with hope by the power of the Holy Spirit" (Romans 15:13).

Step 1: Acknowledge Past Experience

Step 2: Recognize And Feel Feelings

Step 3: Name The Loss

Step 4: Understand The Grief Cycle

Step 5: Challenge Your Beliefs

Step 6: Choose To Forgive

Step 7: Let Go And Live In Today

Step 1

Acknowledge Past Experience

Your experience matters. Acknowledging your past experiences doesn't mean you necessarily like them; it just means you are moving out of denial. Denial holds you back from getting unhooked. Denial tells you that if you don't think about or acknowledge your experience, then it had no impact on you.

The truth is that your past happened. It's part of who you are today. Your experiences do impact you.

Unhooking from your past is about acknowledging and telling your story. You can tell your story through talking, writing, journaling, or creating a song or a poem. The ways to share your story is endless and tailored to who you are. Telling your story moves you out of denial.

 Your story matters. It connects your past to who you are today.

It's easy to live in a fantasy world if you don't talk about what's going on in your life. You live life wearing different masks that are used to cover and hide the pain. Walking out of denial is the first major step toward healing. Until you acknowledge there's something wrong, you can't move forward. Hearing your story in your own voice can take the power away from the impact it once had. It helps you proclaim, "I can walk through this."

Denial keeps you numb, but it doesn't eliminate the pain.

Remember, when you circle around emotional pain (see page 72), you're choosing to believe it's too difficult to face.

When you walk through emotional pain, you're choosing to believe that there's a beginning and a hope for a conclusion to the pain.

Whether or not you work through your emotional pain doesn't change the fact that you have emotional pain.

89

Perhaps you're afraid to walk through pain, telling yourself such things as: "If I deal with this, I'm going to be in too much pain." "I can't face the pain." "I am going to drown in the pain." "This pain is going to kill me." That belief system is false. Yes, it is true that the journey will be difficult, but it will not kill you.

 Instead of moving around the pain, walk *through* it. Although it's intense and hard work, this process has a beginning and an end. And that is what you need!

WHEN YOU DON'T ACKNOWLEDGE YOUR PAST EXPERIENCE

What happens if you choose not to acknowledge your past experience? What are the negative repercussions?

Feeling Crazy

You may begin to feel like you are going crazy, as if there's something wrong with you. As you remain hooked to that past experience, the emotional burden often shows up in depression, anxiety, anger, and addiction. You might feel as if you can't cope, so you isolate yourself. You carry this heavy burden by yourself, and often do so without anyone ever knowing it. As you isolate yourself, you begin to feel more and more unloved. Then you start to feel that you're drastically different from other women around you.

You Ruminate

To ruminate means to dwell on something, thinking about it over and over. It's similar to a cow chewing its cud. The cow will chew and chew and chew, regurgitating the food. That's what it's like when you ruminate on the negativity of your story. It consumes your thinking. It consumes how you focus through the day. You replay the story over and over. There's little room for the regular thoughts of daily life, because you're consumed with the past experience and how painful your life is.

I hold to the belief that you are not responsible for your initial first thought, yet you are responsible for what you do with that thought. Some thoughts just pop into your mind, yet you do have the power and the responsibility to stop the ruminating behavior of those thoughts.

It's not your initial thought that's the main problem. It's what you do with the thought that matters.

If you're a ruminator, you're feeding negative thoughts, which will grow into a defeatest attitude. You need to learn how to starve the negative thoughts and feed positive ones instead. This takes practice. At first, it will seem abnormal to stop yourself and replace negative thoughts with healthy ones. You can replace these negative thoughts with Scripture, an uplifting song, or focus on something positive that will distract you. You need to determine whether what you are thinking about is beneficial to your life.

What you feed grows, and what you starve dies.

my life

I've had some pretty wacky and negative thoughts come to my mind and wondered, "What's wrong with me? How come I have such wacky thoughts?" Often these thoughts came from unresolved stories in my life and the beliefs I had connected to them.

What I discovered is that some thoughts just come. I don't know how, but they come from out of nowhere. I did not have control to prevent the initial thought from coming. What I've learned is that it isn't the initial thought I should feel ashamed about. So often I would feel very terrible about myself because of the thoughts that came into my mind. I learned that I needed to be concerned about what I was going to do with the thought instead. Am I going to feed it if it's negative and damaging? Or, am I going to starve it so it can no longer take space in my mind and heart?

It wasn't until I began to "unhook" from my difficult experiences that I began to recognize that my mind was now less consumed with pain and negativity. Since I had finally acknowledged my past experience and shared my story, I no longer had to find a spot in my mind for the story to dwell.

You Live In Fear And Dread

A third consequence to not sharing your story is living your life in fear and dread that bad things are going to happen. This is often because you don't know there's another way of thinking about the memories of your past experiences. Because of this, you can easily normalize these fearful emotions and begin to believe that when anything difficult happens the outcome will always be dismal.

 Fear and dread don't need to have ownership over you anymore.

Most things in life are not life-threatening. Difficulties, trials, and painful experiences come regularly into our lives. The strategy is to determine if these common life struggles will be given the power to make you feel impending doom. As you learn to put "life stuff" into perspective, and develop an attitude of hope and ownership, the dreadful feelings lose their impact. You begin to live more freely!

WHEN YOU ACKNOWLEDGE YOUR PAST

What can happen if you do acknowledge your past experiences? Let me tell you that good stuff happens when you tell your story.

Talking Makes You Feel Better

I know many women have apprehension about this, but it's the truth: talk therapy is great. Talking makes you feel listened to. It helps you feel there's a relationship between you and someone else.

 Talk therapy is a powerful "medication."

You Realize You're Not Alone

This is a good thing to realize. You can easily feel as if it's impossible that something that happened to you also happened to somebody else. You feel there's no way anyone else can understand what you have been through. I assure you you're not alone. There are thousands of women who have struggled with something similar to you. As I've already mentioned, many women have, sadly, been abused as children. One out of four women has been sexually abused by the age of eighteen. There have been millions of abortions, which means other women also experience regret. It's also important to know that if you've come out of a verbally, emotionally, mentally, spiritually, or physically abusive relationship you're not alone. There are thousands of women who live daily in silence in abusive relationships. Some women have even escaped the relationship and still feel alone.

 As you tell your story, you will realize you are not alone.

Whether one of these experiences has impacted your life, or there's another traumatic experience in your past, there are women who have experienced something similar.

You Expose Lies When You Tell Your Story

There are often numerous lies whirling around in your head that you are not mindful of. Many are not recognizable until you begin to share and compare them with how others see life. You can then become aware that there may be a different way to believe about yourself.

Lie #1: Distorted Self-Worth

One very common lie is holding a distorted sense of self-worth. You might have great difficulty believing in yourself. You need to expose the lie that self-worth comes from how you feel about yourself. Accept that your self-worth comes from the fact you're created in the image of God as a human being.

Don't believe the lie that you are personally responsible for your self-worth. Go back and read the chapter I wrote on "The Biggest Lie Women Believe" if you still struggle with believing in your worth and value.

 Accept the truth that God determines your worth.

Lie #2: I'm Too Bad

Another lie that gets exposed when you tell your story is the one that says, "I'm too bad." It's not about being good or bad. It's about an experience, how it affected you, and how you dealt with it. Yes, you might have dealt with something in an unhealthy way and are now experiencing consequences to your behavior, but that is not the same as being too bad.

 When you feel you're too bad, you're telling yourself that you do not have any hope of making good choices.

Lie #3: I Deserve Punishment

When you expose the lie of "being too bad", you also expose the lie that you deserve to be punished by others. You allow mental, emotional, and relational abuse out of self-loathing. You might feel you need to be punished because you know everything you've done and haven't done throughout your life. You know your weaknesses and often look at them as determinants of who you are and whether or not you should be punished. Even if you don't experience punishment from someone else, you punish yourself, because you're confident you need to be punished. You make decisions and choices based on self-punishment.

In reality, the only one who has the authority to punish you is God. But in His love for you He sent Jesus Christ to take your punishment. Self-inflicted punishment (emotionally, mentally, physically and relationally) only distorts your openness to receiving God's grace in your life.

Lie #4: There's No Hope

Another lie you need to expose is the one that says there's no hope for you. Yes, there is. There's great hope for you! You're a valuable human being who has great potential. You were made by God for a great purpose.

 God didn't make anyone without purpose. This is your hope.

Hope is based on knowing there can be change. When you believe the lie of no hope, you think there can't be change. There can always be change. You can be living proof of it. There's hope until there's no breath. You're breathing anyway, so you might as well look for hope. Seek and find hope.

As you tell your story and expose some of these lies, imagine the power you gain. Lies disintegrate. Your life changes. It's incredible!

my life *All four of these lies are common statements women have shared with me over the years. Yet because these women kept silent with these thoughts, the opportunities to expose these lies were very limited. Too many women have been*

99

deceived by these lies. I was also one of them myself. It always excites me when women have the courage to tell me what they truly believe because that is when the beginning of a new perspective on their future begins. This is when they can begin replacing lies with truth. This puts a smile on my face and a joy in my heart!

Secrets Are Exposed

When you tell your story, secrets are exposed. Secrets imprison people and tell them that they have no hope.

 Secrets kill, steal, and destroy. Secrets have no place in your life.

Exposing a secret isn't an easy thing to do. It takes courage to tell your story. Don't be deceived into believing only weak people talk about their problems.

When you expose a secret, you look at it in the face, and refuse to let it chase you with fear any longer. The secret dissolves.

 A secret is only powerful when it keeps you running.

A secret tells you to never expose anything. It keeps you trapped in the belief that you're worth what happened to you – that you deserved it. A secret says that if you share your story, you'll in turn affect someone else's life negatively. The reality is that you have been hurt by someone else and you're the one who has been affected. Yes, you may expose others by sharing your story, but you'll also stop the cycle of trauma and start a cycle of healing.

 Exposing the secret and sharing your story isn't about retaliation. It's about freedom.

It's learning how to get unhooked from someone who violated you or denied your right to be worthy. The longer the secret is kept, the more the secret can harm you.

 When you keep secrets, you have to tell lies to keep the secret safe.

You build lies to protect yourself and what you're thinking. It's a huge struggle. Yet when secrets are exposed, there's freedom. It's like a filthy rag dropping from you, revealing a fresh cleanness. It relieves a heavy burden.

Your Sense Of Guilt Is Lifted

Walking around with a sense of guilt and shame is a horrible way to live. If you're carrying guilt, it may come out in your life as anger, low self-worth, depression, or an unbalanced drive to succeed.

As you share your story, you will learn how to separate false guilt (condemnation) from true guilt (conviction). (I teach about this topic in greater detail in Step 4). You begin to take responsibility for your own stuff and ditch what is not yours.

Guilt you haven't dealt with is a burden on your shoulders. It feels like you are "carrying the world", which can make you feel crazy and overwhelmed. Telling your story helps you to release the burden because you weren't meant to carry the world on your shoulders. You were only meant to carry your own stuff.

You Honor Yourself

You realize you're valuable. You realize you're worth more than what is happening or has happened. It's loving to honor yourself. You're a valuable human being and you have the right and choice to honor yourself.

When you tell your story, you honor yourself by claiming, "I matter. I matter a lot. I matter because God placed me in this world at this time, in this location, and I matter."

WHO TO TALK TO

 Courageous people talk about their problems.

You might wonder to whom you should tell your story. You might hesitate to share because you think sharing means telling everyone you see and meet. This is not accurate. Although you need to discern who to talk to it is equally important to know who you don't need to talk to.

You should definitely talk to people you can trust. Do you have a close friend, a loving partner, a pastor, a prayer partner, or a counsellor you can seek out?

Although it's not as much about the role a person plays in your life, it is important that you sense you can trust that person. Be discerning. Never share your story with someone you know will share it with someone else unless you are okay with that. Don't share with someone you know to be a gossip, because it's a painful experience to have trust broken again.

 There's nothing weak about asking for help.

It's a sign of strength to have the courage to talk to somebody. Seek someone and get help.

WHEN TO SHARE

If you wonder when you should share, the answer is *now*. Do it now. Don't let your past imprison you anymore. Claim your freedom. Seek to have the very best life possible.

Stop making excuses. You don't know what your future will be or how long you'll be able to make this decision, so begin today to seek the best life possible.

Seek your freedom now! Not a week from now, a month from now, or a year from now. Not when you think you'll have more time, less responsibilities, or more money. You cannot have your best life if you're hooked.

Prayer

Dear God,

Thank you for knowing all about me. Even though my life is not a secret to You, You still love me. Give me the courage to step out and find a place to share my story so I can begin the process of healing.

In Jesus' name,

Amen.

Digging In

Make a list of who you can talk to about your story. Contact someone today.

What secrets are chasing you?

Practice the feeding and starving principle in your life. What lying thoughts do you need to starve and replace with truth?

How have you felt alone in your story?

What excuses are you making as to why you're not walking out of denial?

How is denying the impact of your story keeping you from having a deeper purpose with God?

How many hooks do you have? Give them names.

What secret(s) do you need to expose?

On a scale of 1-10 (10=100%), how much do you feel your story matters? The lower the number the less likely you are to begin the unhooking process.

Can you pinpoint times when you have "gone around" your emotional pain? What was the outcome?

Can you pinpoint times when you have "walked through" your pain (without quitting in the process)? What was the outcome?

How often do you ruminate?

Does ruminating consume your daily activities?

Has your ruminating progressed into anxious thoughts and behaviors? If so, begin to take captive of your ruminating thoughts and seek solutions to each concern.

When was the last time you honored yourself? How did you do it?

Are you living under condemnation? What do you need to do in order to be free from it?

Is there something God is convicting you about that you need to deal with?

In your own words, write what you've learned from this chapter.

His Words Of Hope

✝ "No, in all these things we are more than conquerors through him who loved us" (Romans 8:37).

✝ "Brothers, I do not consider myself yet to have taken hold of it. But one thing I do: Forgetting what is behind and straining toward what is ahead, I press on toward the goal to win the prize for which God has called me heavenward in Christ Jesus" (Philippians 3:13-14).

✝ "And we know that in all things God works for the good of those who love him, who have been called according to his purpose" (Romans 8:28).

✝ "The thief comes only to steal and kill and destroy; I have come that they may have life, and have it to the full" (John 10:10).

✝ "Carry each other's burdens, and in this way you will fulfill the law of Christ" (Galatians 6:2).

Step 2

Recognize And Feel Feelings

Galatians 5:22-23 says, "But the fruit of the Spirit is love, joy, peace, patience, kindness, goodness, faithfulness, gentleness and self-control. Against such things there is no law." If you're hooked with a story that has negatively impacted you, you'll struggle to live by this passage of Scripture. It's difficult because you are afraid to feel feelings.

Experiencing feelings isn't the problem. What we do with those feelings is what causes problems. Jesus felt many things: sadness, disappointment, anger, joy, and passion. So the feelings you have aren't wrong in themselves, but how you react to those feelings might be unhealthy.

Emotions are meant to be experienced - not to harm you. Life without allowing yourself to feel is a lonely way to live. Emotions give you a sense of being alive. They're indicators of deeper things in life. Painful feelings often indicate that either you've been harmed or (perhaps) you have harmed others. Positive feelings often indicate emotional health and a general sense of well-being.

 You don't need to be afraid of negative emotions. You only need to learn how to recognize them, give them space, and then let them go.

When you don't give proper space to your negative emotions, you develop unhealthy ways to cope.

COMMOM UNEAHLTHY WAYS TO COPE

Uncontrolled Behavior

A common way of releasing negative emotions in an unhealthy way is in uncontrolled behavior such as yelling, swearing, or getting physically aggressive toward people or objects. A sudden, overwhelming negative emotional outburst indicates you haven't been dealing with your emotions in a healthy way. You might rationalize uncontrolled behavior, claiming it's not tied to anything, but it's likely a trigger from a past experience you're hooked to, and it's creeping into your present life. (I talk more about anger in Step 4).

Neglecting Depression Symptoms

On the other hand, bottled up emotions have nowhere to go. They churn around in your heart and mind, generally being expressed through depression and isolating behaviors. So instead of aggressive behavior you resort to passive behavior. Some people even neglect their depression to the point of suicide (I talk more about depression in Step 4).

Emotions aren't your enemy. They're your friend. They help you grow and learn.

WHY WE'RE AFRAID OF FEELINGS

What is it about feelings that cause us to wonder if there's something wrong with us? Why are we sometimes so afraid of them?

Unfamiliarity

People are often not familiar with a wide variety of emotions. We know happy, sad, mad, and glad, but how much do we know about all the other emotions? How are these four basic emotions connected to other emotions?

Let me give you some examples. A mad feeling can be connected to being overwhelmed. The deeper emotion of sadness can be connected to feeling a sense of loneliness. Happiness can be connected to a feeling of confidence. Gladness can be tied to being hopeful.

There are many emotions beyond happy, mad, sad, and glad, but these are the basic ones we learn in life. It takes time and work to learn other emotions and put names to them.

 It's vital to your emotional growth to pinpoint what your true emotion is so you can get unhooked.

my life *As I help women figure out what they're feeling beyond happy, mad, sad, and glad, they often have difficulty understanding the many other emotions that exist. I give women a handout containing "feeling faces" and ask them to carry it with them. When they experience an emotion, especially happy, mad, sad, or glad, I ask them look through all the "feeling faces" to determine the deeper and more accurate feeling. If you want to try the same thing, google "feeling faces" images on the internet. You'll find several examples.*

 If you don't understand your emotions, you can easily be afraid of them.

Misunderstanding About Emotions

Another reason we're afraid of feelings is we've been told we shouldn't or can't have certain emotions, especially

117

negative ones. Perhaps people have told you everything will be okay if you keep emotions positive and avoid or ignore the negative ones. "Don't be angry." "Don't be mad." "Don't do that." "Take control of yourself." "Grow up. Stop being a baby."

No wonder you're confused!

Emotions are neither good nor bad. They are just emotions. Remember, it's not about the emotion itself. It's about how you deal with emotions. Perhaps you haven't learned how to respond properly to emotions. You've taught yourself to only react and you find yourself out of your control, so you are often told you're too emotional.

 There is always hope to learn new ways to respond to your feelings instead of react to them.

As you understand and take ownership of your emotions, you will no longer feel out of control or afraid of them.

Fear Of Going Through Your Emotions

Another reason we're afraid of feelings is because we think we might "drown" or "burn" in our pain because the emotions seem so powerful. Sometimes the pain can be so intense you literally feel you could die from it all. You won't. Remember, emotions in themselves can't harm you. You can own them and grow from them.

I want to encourage you to not walk through your pain alone. It's powerful to have someone walking with you. Another person can help you stay balanced in your perspective. They can also comfort you through your tears. Sometimes even having someone to just listen to you can give you the courage to keep working through your healing.

my life *I remember feeling as if I was going to "drown in all the pain" when I started facing my painful past. However, I had someone walking alongside me, encouraging me and helping me understand what I was feeling. I encourage you to have someone walk alongside you as well. And remember, God promises in Isaiah 43:2 that, "When you pass through the waters, I will be with you; and when you pass through the rivers, they will not*

119

sweep over you. When you walk through the fire, you will not be burned; the flames will not set you ablaze".

I've walked alongside many women through the process of working through their emotional pain and each one learns she won't die from the process. You won't either, and when you get to the other side you'll be more aware of who you are. You'll experience freedom.

The 3-Step Action Strategy

Now that you're aware of why you might be afraid of feelings, you can take the next step to set aside your fears, begin to understand your feelings, and make decisions on how you will respond to them. You can dig deeper than happy, mad, sad, and glad and begin to understand why and how you tick, so you are able to unhook from your past.

This 3-Step Action Strategy will help you reflect on what's going on in your life today and strengthen you to take a risk and stop circling around your emotional pain. You'll be ready to choose to walk right through the emotional pain and come out on the other side.

my life *A woman recently said to me, "There's no way I can go through these steps." I encouraged her to get started, and we'd practice them together in counselling. She was still uncertain, but after a couple weeks, she knew the steps and how to apply them.*

When we first met, she shared her tendencies of suicide. She was afraid that if she dealt with her emotions, she'd become suicidal again. I encouraged her to still try because this time she had some new information for how to face her loss, and I was also available if she needed me. (Please note this important statement. If you are feeling suicidal or have suicidal tendencies it is very important that you have a counsellor to help you through your emotional work. Don't try and go it alone for the time being).

The first time she tried these steps on her own, she acknowledged that it was intense. She said it was scary, and she shared how much she cried during the process, but she stayed in her emotions and reflected on what they meant. She proudly stated, "I came out the other side and I know I can do it now." She learned she didn't have to be afraid, because her emotions were no longer her enemy.

Action Strategy 1: Accept Your Feelings

Accept that you are feeling something about an experience. Don't lie to yourself. Be honest about the situation. Lies aren't from God, so when you lie to yourself, you can be certain that what you're thinking isn't from God. It's from Satan, who doesn't want you to grow. Satan doesn't want you to have freedom from your situation. He wants you to pretend you don't have feelings about something, so you minimize the situation, don't deal with it, and stay hooked to it.

Recognize when you're denying or running away from your emotions. Here are some examples of how women have described how they deal with their emotions. Watch for the clues to see if any sound familiar.

Clue #1:

One clue you may be denying your emotions is when you say, "My emotions are all bottled up in me." Imagine taking all your emotions, pushing them into a bottle, and sticking a lid on the bottle so nothing can escape. If you live with bottled emotions you may find yourself confused about what you think and feel. Women often

122

come to counselling when their bottles are pressurized and ready to explode. It's very overwhelming and scary to take off the lid at this time.

Clue #2:

Another way to know you're not accepting your emotions is when you stuff them, which sounds similar to bottling them, but is slightly different. Stuffing is like shoving more and more emotions into a bag. Every now and then you push them down to compact everything, making room for more emotions. When you stuff your emotions too tightly, you won't be able to feel as intensely or accurately. You'll become numb, similar to how people sometimes numb their feelings with alcohol, gambling, or some other addiction.

The result of stuffing your emotions is that you might respond with angry or hurtful outbursts.

Today, even if your bag is so full that it's beginning to tear on the sides, and you're scared to look at what's inside, it's time to deal with them. You'll be okay. It's uncomfortable and scary, but you can begin to walk through your emotional pain.

Clue #3:

Perhaps you continually push down the same emotion, but don't necessarily pack other things on top of it. Basically, you are picking and choosing which emotions you will deal with. When you experience that taboo negative emotion, you push it down, yet it comes back up after a while. This makes you feel uncomfortable. So, you push it down again, wait a while – until it comes back up – then you push it down again. You become overly sensitive in one area of your life.

Clue #4:

You might also sweep emotions under the proverbial rug. You tend to ignore them. You think you can hide the negative emotions from your life. Eventually the rug gets a big hump in it, you start tripping over it, and you have no choice but to look under the rug and clean under it.

You might say, "If I don't think about it, it isn't there." Ignoring something isn't a valid way of dealing with things. It doesn't make the emotions nonexistent.

Perhaps you've used statements such as "It doesn't bother me" or "It's no big deal." When you have to say that, it's usually not true. You're trying to deceive yourself. When you have a "whatever" attitude, there's likely an emotion not being talked about or acknowledged. You're likely disturbed about something, yet you are not talking about it.

You might be afraid, because you know you've been sweeping things under the rug for a long time. Lift the corner and clean one section at a time. You'll have the entire area cleaned up before you know it.

Did you relate to any of these clues? If so, it is time to accept your emotions and face them head on.

 Hurtful things will happen in life. How you respond and deal with them is essential to whether or not you live an unhooked life.

Even if you're very good at hiding your emotions and pretending that everything is fine, things will rise to the surface someday, often in ways and at times you don't expect.

For example, many childhood sexual abuse survivors feel they've worked through the pain until they get married. Then intimacy issues start cropping up. Women want to be loving wives but those past childhood experiences cause emotional triggers which start impacting their lives. Women often don't understand what's going on. These intimacy conflicts can cause major problems in marriage.

Women who have had an abortion might find themselves struggling when they get pregnant again and decide to carry this baby to term. Prior to getting pregnant again, they might have convinced themselves that the abortion didn't significantly impact their lives. However, unresolved conviction and regret torments them and numerous women admit that now there is barely a day that goes by when they do not have thoughts about their aborted child.

Women who have come out of abusive relationships might not seek help, because they're simply relieved to be out of the relationship (which takes a lot of courage). They think the problem was just about the specific individual and that the abuse won't happen again.

However, they begin another relationship and when similar issues start to surface, they find themselves caught up in their old patterns because they haven't dealt with the real issues. Regardless of the specific situation, you might ask, "What's wrong with me?" "Why do I keep bringing the same kind of people into my life?" "Am I bad?" "Do I deserve this?" It's not about you being bad or deserving something. It's about getting unhooked.

Taking ownership of your feelings takes work. You're worth the hard work. Acknowledge what things mean to you. You must deal with things that matter and get unhooked so that you are able to live in the present.

Action Strategy 2: Stay In Your Emotions

In addition to accepting your feelings, the second action step to walking through your emotions involves actually sitting in (or staying in) the emotional feeling for a while. Don't worry: I'm not suggesting a deep trance, primal screaming, or any other extreme response.

Staying in your emotions means learning to be okay with uncomfortable feelings.

Learn how to not run from, suppress, or deny your emotions. Being uncomfortable won't hurt you; it's part of the process of moving through your emotions.

my life *I often speak with women who are afraid to slow down enough to feel something, because they don't want to break down and cry. They think that crying makes them weak or indicates they are immature. Crying often embarrasses them. If you hold a similar belief about the expression of crying, I encourage you to ditch that belief. Crying is a natural overflow of emotional release. Tear ducts were given for a reason!*

I also speak with a number of women who are concerned if they sit in their emotions, all that will come gushing out will be anger. To many women, anger is an unacceptable emotion. The problem with the unwillingness to address their anger is that it will eventually spill out somewhere else — often in places that are damaging to themselves or others. So, it's wiser to intentionally address the anger than allow it to sweep over you in the midst of an explosive situation.

As you learn more about your emotions and begin accepting them, you'll learn emotions are indicators to tell you something about your life. You'll discover what you need in order to learn and grow. You can find freedom if you are willing to stay in the feeling, listen for the meaning of that feeling, and conquer any incorrect belief.

Emotions aren't dangerous. They give you life. Emotions help you to heal, forgive, be courageous, and believe in yourself. Negative emotions show you that there has been harm done to you (real or imagined), or you've harmed someone else. Positive emotions help you to have fullness and wholeness.

When you experience a negative feeling, you have a choice about how you will tackle it. You can feed it or starve it. Remember, what you feed grows, and what you starve dies. You might not get it right every time, but as you practice these steps, you'll begin to keep your day healthy and whole.

When you experience a feeling you're not pleased with, stop to figure out what's triggering you.

Ask questions like the following:

- What am I remembering?

- What am I fearful of?

- What has been said?

- What do I need to do?

Look at your "feeling faces" chart and decide what you're experiencing. Once you pinpoint the emotion, you can work through it, accept it, and move on.

When you learn to stay in your emotions, to listen and learn, and then move on, you own your emotions. You are now the one making the decisions on how you will respond. You now own your emotions instead of your emotions owning you.

It's important that you do not skip over Action Strategy Step 2 of this process or only partially work through it. I find many women are finally naming the emotion stirring

130

in them yet resist the idea of " staying" in it for a time. Some feel "staying" is counter-intuitive to overcoming emotional pain. It is not.

 The power lies in the ability to stay in the feeling so you can take ownership of what will grow from that emotion.

The next time that emotion is experienced, you will have the upper hand over its impact. How great would that be for you?

Action Strategy 3: Learn How To Let Go

If you want to overcome the fear of feeling your emotions, there is a third action strategy you must implement. In addition to the first action of accepting your emotions, and second action of staying in your emotions, you also need to learn how to let go of your emotions. Don't hang on to negative emotions once you have a good sense of what it is and how it could possibly impact you. Move on.

You move on by resisting the urge to mull over or ruminate the story or experience. Ruminating will keep you stuck. Since you have already applied the two previous action strategies, there is no reason to rehook yourself again. There is no need to give the story any more space in your thinking. This is again where the feeding and starving principle comes into play. If the thoughts or feelings keep trying to invade your thinking, just remind yourself that you have already dealt with the issue and refuse to feed it ammunition.

This is a simple principle yet one of the more difficult action strategies to implement, because you need to train yourself to be actively conscious of what you are thinking. That way, you can intercept any faulty thoughts that try to settle in. At first it can be very mentally tiring because you are still discerning between healthy and unhealthy thinking patterns. Yet over time, the habit of ruminating over a situation will subside if you are persistent with resisting.

What will happen is that you will eventually come to discover that a majority of the time your mind is no longer filled up with negative and worrisome thoughts because you have already dealt with the emotion. It sure feels good to have space in your mind for positive and freeing thoughts!

my life *I can remember what it was like to be paralyzed for two or three days in a row when my emotions took hold of me. I've wasted days in the grip of what I thought was a powerful emotion. Yet, I've also learned that when I understand the feeling, put a meaning with it, and give it space, I can let it go.*

Perhaps I'd wake up mad. I wouldn't know why, and I often wouldn't take the time to examine the why. As the day progressed, I'd feed that mad feeling, taking it out on my family or anyone else around me. I was out of control and no one knew what to say to me to make it right. I didn't even know what to say to myself.

As I learned to apply the 3-Step Action Strategy, my response to my life situations changed drastically. I still use this strategy on a regular basis throughout my day. It has tremendously freed up my life!

Prayer

Dear God,

Help me to not be afraid of emotions. Give me the courage to walk through my emotional pain, knowing that You are beside me all the way. Teach me how to respond to all my emotions in healthy ways.

In Jesus' name,

Amen.

Digging In

What were you taught in regards to emotions?

What names were you called by others when you showed your emotions?

What feelings do you think are "bad"?

To what degree were you given permission to talk through your emotions?

In what situations do you lie to yourself in regards to how you feel about something?

Have you ever felt like you were drowning in your feelings? If so, what did you do to keep afloat? Have your strategies been healthy or unhealthy?

Describe, or draw, how you "store" the emotions you have not dealt with (bottle, stuff, push down, etc.).

At what number do you treat yourself? (10=100% valuable, 1= 0% valuable)

How do you allow yourself to be emotionally uncomfortable?

How would life change if you owned your emotional responses?

How often do you practice being aware of your emotions?

How often do you practice being aware of your thoughts?

In your own words, write what you've learned from this chapter.

His Words Of Hope

† "Cast all your anxiety on him because he cares for you" (1 Peter 5:7).

† "You will keep in perfect peace him whose mind is steadfast, because he trusts in you" (Isaiah 26:3).

† "We demolish arguments and every pretension that sets itself up against the knowledge of God, and we take captive every thought to make it obedient to Christ" (2 Corinthians 10:5).

† "But the fruit of the Spirit is love, joy, peace, patience, kindness, goodness, faithfulness, gentleness and self-control. Against such things there is no law" (Galatians 5:22-23).

† "Do not repay evil with evil or insult with insult, but with blessing, because to this you were called so that you may inherit a blessing" (1 Peter 3:9).

Step 3

Name The Loss

So often putting a name to our loss can be healing. Naming the secondary losses is one step that I feel is often overlooked in the healing process. Very few women I have talked to have even heard about the idea of working through the impact of secondary losses that may have resulted due to a traumatic experience. Because of this, it seems numerous women do not feel they have accomplished a deep sense of healing. Instead, they state they only feel a partial sense of release from the affects of the past.

As you get started, I just want to encourage you not to skip over Step 3 of the *Unhooked!* process. I recognize this step might be time consuming and emotionally draining, yet it is vital for you to process it in order to move towards complete healing.

In this chapter, I outline possible secondary losses you may be experiencing if you've been sexually abused as a child, had an abortion, or have been in some sort of relational abuse. I recognize that I will not be able to cover all of the possible secondary losses, as the list is vast, and there may be a very *specific* loss you are experiencing due to the fact that each individual's loss is personal to each life situation.

Instead, I focus on some the more common examples of secondary losses that women have shared with me. I include more detail in regards to the actual "unhooking" process in the last half of the chapter.

Although this chapter focuses on the losses that may occur for a woman who has been sexually abused as a child, had an abortion, or have been in some form of relationship abuse, I want you to know that you can transfer the same principles of understanding secondary losses to any situation you have experienced, so you can follow the same path towards healing as any other woman.

WHAT ARE SECONDARY LOSSES?

With every negative experience, there comes a loss. Loss doesn't come only with death, although that's primarily what we consider when we think of losses. Loss comes from many experiences, and with every primary loss, there are always secondary losses.

The primary loss looks more tangible than the secondary loss. It's the major loss, so that is what you focus on most. You'll often not dig deeply enough to discover and define the secondary losses. For example, in the areas in which I frequently counsel – childhood sexual abuse, abortion, and relational abuse – we know the major loss is in those actual experiences. However, there are many other losses that occur in connection with the primary loss, yet they aren't as easily recognized or focused upon.

Some women struggle with the loss of a sense of self-worth, the ability to trust, permission to hope, desire to live motivated, and the courage to risk. I'm only scratching the surface of what secondary losses look like. They also include losses to relationships, values, and even material things. Secondary losses can feel like a huge weight, keeping you hooked to your past. You need to identify them.

 Secondary losses are natural consequences due to a primary loss.

There is a consequence to every action in life. Sometimes it's a positive consequence, and sometimes it's a negative consequence. Consequences are a normal outflow of loss. However, it is very important to note that secondary loss consequences are not the same as punishments, even though people often interpret them as such.

For example, when life is tough for a woman who has experienced childhood sexual abuse, had an abortion, or have been in an abusive relationship, she can easily interpret difficult aspects of her life as punishment. She might say, "I'm a bad person. If I was a good person, I wouldn't be having this experience."

 Numerous women truly believe that God is putting obstacles and pain in their paths as a way to punish them.

That's not a true belief. There are some experiences in life that are just natural outcomes or consequences of a previous action. It's important to recognize it's not punishment that is causing the pain; it is consequences. Sometimes the consequence is due to your actions, and unfortunately, some consequences you experience are due to another's action against you. Regardless of who is responsible, you will experience secondary losses because of it. When you experience a loss, your life changes.

Ask yourself the following questions:

- How has my life changed?

- What happened in my life?

- What are some of the secondary losses I recognize from my experiences?

143

- What changes are a direct result of how I have lived my life?

- What are some of the things in my life that have changed because of this traumatic experience?

 You don't need to feel bad about where you've been or where you are. There is hope.

Yet if you don't examine the painful things in your life, you cannot get well. It's like a sliver in your thumb. If you ignore the sliver, it festers. You might not notice it much until you suddenly bump it against something. The pain shoots through your hand and up your arm. That's what happens when you don't deal with your secondary losses. That sliver of loss is hidden and festers until you bump into the story again and you can't ignore it any longer.

SECONDARY LOSSES IN CHILDHOOD SEXUAL ABUSE

The primary loss a person experiences from childhood sexual abuse is the right to have full ownership over her body. Someone has violated that right and determined that they had a greater right. They stole that person's

144

ownership. Along with this primary loss, numerous secondary losses come into play.

Loss Of Sense Of Purity

Purity is how you feel about yourself sexually. The opposite of feeling pure is feeling dirty. When you're made to feel dirty about yourself at an early age, you're not even old enough to recognize and challenge the belief so you could change it. As you become a teenager, you might act out by being promiscuous or by participating in sexual things you wouldn't have done otherwise. You believe you're already dirty, so you start living out what you feel.

Loss Of Trust

Another secondary loss due to sexual abuse is that of trust. Trust is broken by whomever harmed you when you were a child. In turn, a general lack of trust for people is carried throughout your life. You learn to keep people at arm's length, not letting them totally into your life.

As with many secondary losses, you might not easily recognize you're dragging the weight of distrust around with you. You may describe your behavior as boundary-setting instead. However, when you struggle with trust issues, you will often find yourself sabotaging relationships and opportunities. Because of your pain, you struggle to believe life or people can be different.

Loss Of Self-Worth

It's amazing how many women haven't connected their sense of low self-worth with their childhood sexual abuse. Many women believe the experience no longer affects them because it happened so long ago. Sometimes closure has not taken place because the person who abused you is dead, or for some reason, the individual won't be exposed, so your story stays buried.

If you don't directly connect your abuse to a sense of low self-worth you might try insufficient ways to believe in yourself. Yet at the end of the day, you still continue to say, "I'm not worthy".

Now we're back to the 10/10 principle. Even though you might rate yourself low or negative on a scale of 1 to 10, it's important to recognize your self-worth comes from God, not yourself and your life experiences. The greatest growth comes when you choose to believe this truth and live with respect for yourself.

Someone may have attempted to deny you of your value by violating that boundary, but you do not have to accept that anymore!

Loss Of Positive Intimacy

Another secondary loss to sexual abuse is loss of positive intimacy with your husband. If you haven't worked through your sexual abuse, it will probably be triggered during times of intimacy, including basic non-sexual touching. Although your reaction is not intentional, you likely haven't made the connection between childhood sexual abuse, how your desire for intimacy is affected, and how these conflicts can come between the two of you.

It's important to talk with your husband about how you are being triggered. Otherwise, it's possible he'll feel punished for something someone else did, even if you're not intentionally trying to punish him. You might need to involve someone else, like a good friend or counsellor, to help you walk through the process together. As husband

and wife together, it is okay to want intimacy to be a beautiful part of your marriage.

Loss Of Respect For Men

Loss of respect for men is a common secondary loss. Without even realizing it, you might assign lack of general respect to all men by putting them in the same category with the man who abused you. One way to recognize this issue is to be aware of your overall anger towards men. Do you feel threatened, judged, or in competition with men? Even if the feeling is subtle, it can impact nearly all your male relationships.

Obviously this list of secondary losses isn't complete but includes some of the common losses women experience. Pay close attention to how your experiences have impacted your life. Acknowledge and get unhooked from secondary losses resulting from your childhood sexual abuse.

SECONDARY LOSSES IN RELATIONAL ABUSE

The primary loss of relational abuse is the inability to have a stable, healthy, and fulfilling love relationship with your partner. Even so, secondary losses of relational abuse might not be readily recognizable, so it's important to know some possible signs.

Loss Of Choice

Having the power to make your decisions as an adult is imperative to a mature and stable lifestyle. Generally, if you are in an abusive relationship and are being manipulated or abused mentally, emotionally, spiritually, or physically, you likely assume that you don't have any choices in life. You might feel or believe you're stuck. You might even be afraid to make choices, fearful you'll make a wrong choice, which will lead to retaliation from your partner.

Loss Of Focus

Another secondary loss is the ability to focus. You might be living in such deep fear that it affects your ability to focus on everyday life, because much of your time is spent trying to feel safe or trying to keep your home a

149

safe place. You're focused on not upsetting your partner, so you can't focus on your life. You live in fear and confusion.

Loss Of Decision-Making

The longer you stay in an abusive relationship, the more you are being forced to rely on your partner to make decisions for you. Consequently, even when you're out of the abusive relationship, you consistently seek the support of other people for assurance or permission about situations in your life. When you're encouraged to make a decision, you might hesitate, thinking, "Should I do this?" "What if I make the wrong decision?" "What if I make a mistake?" Your lack of self-trust is paralyzing you from growing.

Loss Of Self

Another secondary loss that comes from being in an abusive relationship, and is often combined with loss of decision-making, is the loss of self. You may be at a point where you no longer know what you used to believe about most things.

A common statement I hear from women in abusive relationships is "I don't know who I am anymore."

If you hear yourself claiming you don't know who you are anymore, you need to recognize just how impactful the relational abuse has been (whether it's mental, physical, spiritual, or emotional). Once you've been stripped of who you are, you gravitate towards feeling hopeless and useless. This is a very dangerous and unhealthy state to be in, as depression and self-harming behavior could result.

Loss Of Income And Education

Perhaps you've been forbidden to earn income or further your education. You've lost the ability to develop your skills. When you leave the abusive relationship, you may feel lost, because you don't know how you'll earn money. You might be too intimidated to go back to school, because you've been told repeatedly you're not smart enough. You might be fearful to find a job, because you question whether you have the ability or the permission to make money that will be yours to keep. It takes a great deal of courage to step back into the work or education world.

Loss Of Confidence In Parenting

Loss of confidence in parenting is another secondary loss. You might ask yourself, "What kind of a mom was I to have stayed in that relationship?" You've lost the belief that you're capable of good parenting. Even if there seems to be obvious proof that your children are doing well, you might have intense guilt for staying in an abusive relationship for such a long time.

If you can relate to any of these suggested secondary losses, you are not alone. The reality is that many women stay in an abusive relationship because they are afraid of facing these secondary losses. However, now is the time to start dealing with your secondary losses, so you can get out of the relationship, or begin to "find yourself" again, if you have already moved on from the unhealthy situation.

SECONDARY LOSSES FROM ABORTION

The primary loss of abortion is two-fold. The primary loss for the unborn child is that he or she was not given life. The primary loss for the woman who chose abortion is the loss of the opportunity to bring her child into the world and parent that child. This may be the only aspect of loss focused upon, yet there are numerous other losses to be aware of.

Loss Of Self-Respect

If you've had an abortion, you most likely are experiencing the secondary loss of self-respect, which can be amplified if you had previously been against abortion. It's not an uncommon story to hear women say that they were against abortion until they were faced with an unplanned pregnancy. They often share that it was a terrible experience. It was against everything they believed.

When you lose your self-respect, it can lead to you living in an undignified manner. You may do and say things you would never have considered being a part of, because you no longer feel you have the right to think highly of yourself.

Loss Of Control

Perhaps you also feel a loss of control, especially if you were coerced or convinced into having the abortion. You may respond to this loss by expressing anger, dominant behavior, and extreme independence.

Loss Of Peace

There is also a loss of peace. You can't forget you've been pregnant and you are often reminded of this when you see a pregnant woman or newborn baby. There's a sense of unrest in your heart. It's difficult for you to find peace. You know you took the life of another person, and reconciling that in your heart can seem impossible. Yet, by accepting God`s forgiveness, you can bring the peace into your life that you need.

Loss Of Conceiving Again

Sometimes abortion causes the loss of the ability to conceive again. This isn't a punishment for having the abortion; it's a natural consequence of a medical procedure. There are risks in any medical procedure, and one of the risks of abortion is not being able to conceive or carry a child to term. This is a secondary loss that is difficult to unhook. It affects you every time you're trying to conceive.

Loss Of Trust

Perhaps you feel you were lied to as you made decisions about your pregnancy. You didn't fully understand the development of the baby and possible after-affects of abortion. You were told half-truths and not fully informed about all the choices. You might continue to carry a mistrust of people, because you've been deceived.

I trust this overview of potential secondary loss issues helps you identify some of the hooks you may be experiencing in your life. In the rest of this chapter, I provide details of how you can begin unhooking from your secondary losses. Keep in mind that Step 3 of *Unhooked!* is only one component of the healing process. You will see how working through this step will be foundational for working through the next four steps.

155

RESTORATION:
UNHOOKING FROM SECONDARY LOSSES

In Step 3, the goal isn't to simply recognize the connection between the primary and secondary losses.

 The goal is to work through a restoration process and get unhooked.

Through the restoration process keep in mind that you have established many beliefs about your secondary losses, as well as beliefs about yourself, others, life, the future, and God. All these beliefs determine how you interpret the meaning behind your experience of secondary losses.

Much of how you interpreted your experiences as a child filter into how you interpret life as an adult. What if the negative messages you received from your primary experiences and secondary losses are misinterpretations of your core beliefs about who you are? What impact does that have on how you're living life? How skewed might your perspective be in who you are and how you're moving forward in your life?

It's important to recognize what skewed perspectives you might hold so you know exactly what to get unhooked from.

As you work toward restoration it is necessary for you to realize that even though you likely have a combination of past (or present) stories, you can't fix them all at once. It's important that you work on only one story at a time. You need to learn how not to rabbit trail.

For example, let's say you want to address the impact of your childhood sexual abuse story. You share a bit about the actual story and then begin to talk about how it's affecting your marriage. Then you start adding how conflictual your relationship seems to be with your mother. By the end of your conversation, you are acknowledging your fear of overprotecting your nine year old daughter.

Do you see how there are four stories tied into one? It is not uncommon to address your life issues as a whole (because they really are all intertwined) yet it can be counter-productive to focus on all of these issues at once. It is interesting how often a woman will sidetrack back to

157

other issues while in counselling. You need to be aware of this as you work through your story on your own.

I help women identify the separate stories and encourage them to "put aside" the present struggles, just for now, and only focus on their past story. Eventually, the present situations will be identified within the secondary loss consequences. For example, the overprotectiveness could be connected to a timing of a similar age when your abuse happened. Or perhaps the conflictual relationship with your husband could be, in part, due to intimacy problems because you are experiencing triggers whenever he desires sex. So you see, the present situations will be addressed, just not quite yet. You will get a clearer picture of what I am saying as you progress through all the *Unhooked!* steps.

It takes time and effort to identify and separate the stories of your life, so you will need to go through the following steps for *each* story and their corresponding secondary losses. Just be sure to take one story at a time so you can completely unhook from each one.

If you try to unhook several stories at the same time, you'll likely feel you're never getting anywhere and you will want to quit working towards your healing.

THE LOSS PIE PROCEDURE

my life *The following exercise I am going to give you is what I commonly ask women to do as they work toward discovering and identifying what stories and beliefs have them hooked. I use a pie diagram because the visual picture helps me grasp things. You can use any type of outlining that works for you. The pie itself is not the important thing; it's what you write in it that counts.*

Draw a large circle like a pie on a piece of paper. I call this the Loss Pie. Break the pie into as many slices as it's going to take for you to deal with the secondary losses in your particular story.

For example, consider childhood sexual abuse. In the previous section of this chapter, I listed possibly five secondary losses, so if you feel you've experienced all five of them, you'd divide the pie into five sections and write one loss in each section. It's important to sincerely search out what your losses are. You may have more than these

159

five, some may not fit at all, or you may have different ones. Just write them all. If you're not certain, or you think something sounds off the wall, write it down anyway.

The point to dividing the pie into the secondary losses is to help you have appreciation for why you shouldn't attempt to eat the whole Loss Pie at once. You need to be able to take *each* secondary loss separately and understand it's impact on your life. You want to determine what you lost in each particular area. In a further step, you will be making decisions about what losses you can regain.

One very important step is to allot a percentage to the impact you feel the secondary losses have had on you. Let's say the loss of trust was a secondary loss you experienced from your childhood sexual abuse trauma, yet you feel it only holds 20% of your overall "hook." You make the slice 20% out of 100%. That leaves you with 80% of the Loss Pie left for other secondary losses (from this trauma) to be explored. Do this with each secondary loss identified.

Your pie will not likely look symmetrical as you assign percentages. You may have 20% for one loss, 30% for another, 35% for yet another, and 10% and 5% for the remaining ones. However, your Loss Pie may be 50% and 50% (because you only identified two equal losses from your story). That's not a problem. Just be certain your Loss Pie sections total 100% for the whole pie.

Determining the percentages helps you grasp which areas of loss likely have deeper hooks. It also helps you decide which secondary loss you may want to work on first.

my life *It's interesting to see how women divide their pies. First they feel weird about the whole thing, because they haven't taken the time to think about their stories in this way. They may also be afraid of making a mistake in judgment.*

Of course, I always remind each woman that this is not a test and there is no right and wrong. This was her experience, not anyone else's. Besides, she can always readjust her percentages whenever she needs to.

Once you've completed this section and decided which secondary loss to focus on, you might be asking, "Okay, so how do I process this information now?"

Take one secondary loss of your Loss Pie that you have chosen and begin being your own journalist by asking who, what, when, where, why and how questions. For example, in the area of trust you might ask, "Who is responsible for my trust being lost?" You might be surprised to discover that you do not often allot 100% to the perpetrator. Sometimes you might allot a percentage to your parents for not protecting you as you feel they should have. You may allot some of the blame to yourself – determining that you should have told someone about the abuse. Or you may discover it was other people or even organizations that had violated your trust.

Here are some ideas on how you can formulate the questions:

- What did it mean to….?
- How did I feel when…?
- How did…. change how I see myself?

- How can I gain back...?

- When do I feel most triggered by...?

- Who is truly responsible for this ...?

- What beliefs can I challenge about this story?

- Who else should be added into this Loss Pie?

- Why is this emotion coming up now ?

Do this step with *each* secondary loss you identified on your Loss Pie.

This is where the deep work comes into play. This is where you really touch the core of your beliefs, sadness, anger, and eventually, your hope. I will warn you: bring a lot of tissue with you. God is going to do a great healing in your life through this exercise. Pray and ask the Holy Spirit to reveal to you those aspects of the story you need to be aware of.

Please do not be afraid of this process. God is with you. Remember, your story is just that: a story. It is not actually being relived as you work through it, it is only being replayed. You own the speed and depth in which you will process the pain and loss. Do your own digging

163

and ask all the questions you need to until you feel you have exhausted them all.

my life

It is not uncommon for a woman to redo her pie division throughout the healing journey. Remember this is a journey, and you will not get through your story in one sitting. There are numerous layers to peel back. Some are thin and are easily pulled away. Others are thick and cumbersome to release. That's okay. The healing is a process. It's your process. Feel free to de-layer only as much as you are ready to, as often as you need to.

Just a side note: You can use this pie strategy for more than just examining secondary losses. You can use it to determine any emotions that you have: what your anger is made up of, or what your depression is made of, or any other emotion you may be experiencing. Overall, this visual strategy is simply used to give you a better understanding of the components that are impacting your particular experience or emotion.

TAKING BACK WHAT WAS STOLEN

I will now explain the steps you can take to regain some of the emotional losses that were stolen or stunted due to your traumatic experience. As an adult, you have the ability to choose to *not* believe the "hooks" you held as a child. For example, keeping with the childhood sexual abuse theme, you can now question the validity of the meaning of the loss. Be specific in your responses such as, "What I lost because of my sexual abuse was the trust and belief that my partner has the best in mind for me."

Now you've discovered one belief you hold because of the loss of trust. You now have a better understanding of why you are responding to your husband the way you are. This also means you have a better opportunity of doing something about it!

 It's important to look at what you feel you lost through your eyes as an adult, and not through your eyes when you were a child.

You had very little power as a child, so there are perspectives you held back then that you could not have changed at such a young age. But now that you are an adult, you have the power of choice to re-evaluate what meaning your past trauma has permission to hold over

165

you. In other words, what hooks are you allowing yourself to keep?

This is the next vital step to getting unhooked. Ask yourself, "Do I have to believe that because someone violated me, it means I can't trust my husband for the rest of my life?" No it doesn't! Now that you're an adult, you can differentiate between your experience as a child, and your relationships as an adult (I talk more about this in Step 5: Challenge Your Beliefs).

Let me give you another example of how to work through this step. If you have intimacy issues with your husband because you've been sexually abused in the past, your common response to him might be to push him away every time he tries to be intimate with you. You may get into arguments because he may feel confused and hurt. Even though you may try to explain that the lack of desire for intimacy is not about him, you may not be sure what it's all about or how to get past it.

This is a good time to consider, "What did I lose from the abuse?" It is possible that you lost the ability to believe that you can be free in intimacy with your partner. Now, as an adult, you can go back and unhook yourself. You need to ask yourself: "Does this experience have the right and power to tell me I can never be fully free in my intimacy with my husband, whom I love?" You answer will be "No!" You can unhook the belief that sex is cold or dirty or whatever else you believe. You can declare the belief is not true. Instead, you can focus your thoughts and desires on what a legitimate, healthy sexual relationship looks like in marriage and reach for it.

This is how you would evaluate every belief you hold in regards to all your secondary losses. Decide you no longer have to hold to views that steal positive outcomes in your life.

Using the Loss Pie, you'll determine what all the losses are as you work through them one at a time. If you try to "eat" the whole pie at once, you'll feel overwhelmed. However, if you take each piece one at a time, you'll eventually discover you've eaten the entire pie. You'll have your life back. You'll begin to notice that instead of responding with "I can't because of what happened to me," you'll replace your thinking with a positive response, such as, "Yes, I can. I can have my life back now."

 As you walk through the loss, you're not bringing up any feelings that are not already there.

You're just acknowledging them, so you can take ownership and get your life back.

Of course as you're working through the restoration process, you need to be realistic about what you can gain back and what you can't. You can gain back a great deal although you can't gain everything back. For example, if you feel you lost your childhood, you know you can't become a child again. Your body grew and won't become childlike again, but there's no reason why you can't regain a childlike joy. That's a realistic hope.

If something happened to you sexually, can you gain back your virginity? No, but you can certainly gain your sense of purity back. As you bring everything to Jesus, you can know God has cleansed you of anything that would make you feel unworthy. That is what God does for you.

Starting today, you can begin to know that you can be pure from the inside out. That's realistic.

Can you gain back lost time? No, but you can invest in the present and future. The past is the past. Today is today. Tomorrow is tomorrow. Remember, you're no longer looking at this from a child's perspective. You're an adult. You have choices, and you can reclaim what time you have. That's realistic.

If you've had an abortion, you can't get back your baby, but you can have the peace of knowing your baby is safe with God now. Post-abortive support groups are an excellent source of help for the emotional fall-out of abortion. Women find peace even though they're not able to bring back their babies. That is a realistic hope.

 Although you don't forget the memories of something tragic or traumatic that has happened to you, you can have the memory without the pain attached.

The pain of the memory can be slowly lessened so that it doesn't force itself into your thinking every day, consuming you.

I just want you to know that there is something you can gain no matter what your primary or secondary losses have been: Jesus' hope, peace, joy, and truth. Start seeking right now. Don't be afraid. Life is too short to be afraid to seek support. You don't want to let your primary story blind you from recognizing the secondary losses that are holding you down. I want you to have hope today.

 Secondary losses can control your life, but they don't have to. Get help. Get unhooked, because you have a full life waiting for you.

Prayer

Dear God,

I know there are numerous secondary losses due to my past experiences. Thank you that I have permission to gain my life back in spite of what was taken from me. Help me to choose hope today. In Jesus' name,

Amen.

Digging In

Mark any of these secondary losses you feel you've experienced:

Secondary Losses From Sexual Abuse:

☐   Loss of Purity

☐   Loss of Trust

☐   Loss of Self-Worth

☐   Loss of Positive Intimacy

☐   Loss of Respect for Men

Secondary Losses From Relational Abuse:

☐   Loss of Choice

☐   Loss of Focus

☐   Loss of Decision-Making

☐   Loss of Self

☐   Loss of Income and Education

☐   Loss of Parenting

Secondary Losses From Abortion:

☐   Loss of Dignity

☐   Loss of Control

☐   Loss of Peace

☐   Loss of Conceiving Again

☐   Loss of Trust

What are any other secondary losses? Name them all (don't worry about whether they seem too small or insignificant – they are losses to you).

What natural consequence have you experienced, believing it was a form of punishment?

On a scale of 1-10 (10=100%), how willing are you to pursue the hard work to get free from secondary losses?

Have you worked through the process of the Loss Pie? If not, what is keeping you from dealing with your secondary losses?

On a scale of 1-10 (10=100%), how much power do you believe you have over your belief systems?

What is stopping you from choosing to change your belief systems?

In your own words, write what you've learned from this chapter.

His Words Of Hope

† "Why are you downcast, O my soul? Why so disturbed within me? Put your hope in God, for I will yet praise him, my Savior and my God" (Psalm 42:5).

† "Come to me, all you who are weary and burdened, and I will give you rest" (Matthew 11:28).

† "You will keep in perfect peace him whose mind is steadfast, because he trusts in you. Trust in the LORD forever, for the LORD, the LORD, is the Rock eternal" (Isaiah 26:3-4).

† "'For I know the plans I have for you,' declares the LORD, 'plans to prosper you and not to harm you, plans to give you hope and a future'" (Jeremiah 29:11).

† "So do not fear, for I am with you; do not be dismayed, for I am your God. I will strengthen you and help you; I will uphold you with my righteous right hand" (Isaiah 41:10).

Step 4

Understand The Grief Cycle

Grief is a common emotion associated with loss. Grief and loss go hand in hand. People often refer to grief in terms of steps, transitions, or a cycle. I refer to parts of grief as "components," because grieving seldom follows one exact direction or specific order. You'll go through the components of grief, but the intensity, duration, and order will differ from situation to situation and person to person.

You've probably heard many terms associated with grief: shock, denial, anger, guilt, and depression. Some people also include bargaining and loneliness. There's also hope and acceptance. You likely won't experience every aspect exactly the same as someone else, but somewhere in the process of grieving, you'll experience each aspect to some degree.

How you grieve is personal, because loss is personal. No one needs to tell you how you should grieve. How intensely you grieve is your personal experience, because it's about your personal loss. However, there are guidelines and examples to help us identify what's healthy and unhealthy through the grieving process.

 Grieving in and of itself is not unhealthy. It's natural.

You might feel afraid to grieve in your community, because expression of emotion can be scary and overwhelming. When something tragic happens, you're often required to get back to your daily life in a few days, and you're not always given the opportunity to talk about it.

Grief is often associated with death, but you don't need to experience a death in order to have a loss. Loss comes from anything that has been taken from you. Women who have been sexually abused as children, have had an abortion, or have come out of emotionally or mentally abusive relationships experience forms of loss.

 Loss can be the death of something, not just the death of someone.

You might work through the grief components quite quickly, or it might be painstakingly slow and very deep. The length of time isn't so much a problem, although there are some accepted boundary time lines that suggest it is unhealthy if grieving doesn't progress after several weeks. If grief isn't progressing, something else is likely happening. But in general, it's not about how long you grieve, but whether or not you're stuck in one of the components of grieving. It's about the "stuckness of grief."

As you learn more about the components of grief, keep in mind any area in which you might get, or are presently, stuck. Components include shock/denial, anger, guilt, depression, and hope. Hope is similar to acceptance, but you might struggle with the term acceptance, thinking it's something you have to get past. Hope is something you look forward to.

SHOCK/DENIAL

Shock and denial occur when you are in a state of disbelief that the experience is really happening to you (or has happened to you in the past). Denial isn't about denying the experience exists. You know what you've experienced. It's the reason for the grief and loss. You wouldn't have grief and loss without the experience. It is the struggle to acknowledge how much the experience has impacted you.

 Denial is struggling to admit something has changed because of the experience.

One sign indicating that you might be in denial is when you "don't want to talk about it," especially if you have never talked to anybody yet, and don't ever plan to talk to anyone. I realize some women are more private than others and do not have that "gift for gab" as others do. Yet when you try to keep grief completely to yourself, you're probably in the denial component of grief and loss.

Another example would be if you tell yourself it's "no big deal". This is a common statement I hear from women who are stuck in their past stories. I want to suggest that traumatic experiences are a big deal. Hiding behind this statement is a way of protecting yourself from pain.

 Denial is fear that if you touch the pain, it will flood you.

You might decide to stay in denial so you can avoid active grieving. Active grieving is allowing yourself to go through the components of grief. The problem is that when you bottle feelings up for too long and then you finally decide to walk out of denial, your grief seems insurmountable when it begins to come out. That is why I encourage women to start working on their stories sooner rather than later.

Perhaps you've been taught to "suck it up" or "have a stiff upper lip" as you were growing up. There was no approval given for showing your emotions. These lessons make it more likely that you will struggle to move out of denial. The former lack of permission paralyzes women from wanting or trusting help.

Perhaps you've heard someone say, "Be more mature." "Be an adult." "Grow up. You're not a kid anymore." People say these things out of a fear of grief. Growing up doesn't solve all problems. Adults have problems, and they need help to figure them out.

Counselling is still taboo for many people who have been taught they should be able to deal with everything on their own. Yet, you can't know it all, especially when you haven't been taught some things as you were growing up. When something hasn't been modeled for you, it's more difficult to learn.

If you revisit Step One of *Unhooked!* you'll see a connection to denial. When you walk through your story, you step out of denial and move into healthy grieving.

Revisit the emotional pain exercise on page 72. Remember, emotional pain will be there even if you go around and around it, avoiding and denying it. It's always just a thought away. Emotional pain is also there as you go through it and get help to get to the other side.

 Denial fools you into thinking that if you aren't dealing with your story, you don't have the pain.

That's not true. The emotional pain is still there.

GUILT

Guilt is feeling responsible for an offense. You, like many others, likely struggle to discern between false guilt (condemnation) and true guilt (conviction). Of course, there are times when you truly are guilty.

True guilt (conviction) is when you've done something offensive to someone else, yourself, or to God.

What you experience when you go against God's guidelines is true guilt or healthy shame. However, when someone else has harmed you and you carry that burden, believing you're responsible for it (often because someone told you you're responsible for it), you're experiencing false guilt or unhealthy shame.

False guilt is condemnation. Condemnation comes from Satan. It doesn't come from God, as He doesn't condemn people. God, through the Holy Spirit, convicts of sin (true guilt) but never condemns the individual (false guilt).

Satan wants condemnation to keep you from going to God. Condemnation turns things inward, so you begin to build secrets and believe lies of how horrible you are or how you're responsible for everything negative in your life. Negative self-talk is very powerful when you're carrying around false guilt.

False guilt (condemnation) keeps you stuck in your past.

If you're stuck right now, weighed down by guilt that is causing you to look inward and hate yourself, you can be certain you are carrying around something that isn't from God.

True guilt is conviction from God. When you know you've done something truly inappropriate, even if it might be difficult to go to God and make things right, responding to true conviction will draw you closer to God. James 4:8a says, "Come near to God and He will come near to you." True conviction prompts you to want to ask for forgiveness so you experience freedom. You gain hope. False guilt (condemnation/unhealthy shame) pulls you away from God, keeps you stuck, and tells you that there is no hope.

When you are truly convicted, you learn you don't need to degrade yourself; no matter what you're confessing to the Lord, or making right with somebody. Accept the grace of God with confidence, because without His grace,

185

you can't be free. Unhook from it to move into the very best life possible.

 With false guilt (condemnation), you cannot fully grasp grace, and you can't move forward in life. True guilt (conviction) will help you move forward.

I want to remind you again: It's important to examine whether you're experiencing false or true guilt. You need to figure out what you're responsible for, so you can deal with it and move forward. Anytime you've been harmed emotionally, mentally, physically, or spiritually by another person, it's not your guilt to carry. It's their guilt you are carrying. If you were abused as a child, you might wonder, "If only I'd done this or that..." Stop and let go of those statements. You did nothing wrong. You have no guilt to carry.

Of course, if you are carrying true guilt, you need to have the courage to take it to God so you can be forgiven and free. Numerous women who have had an abortion are fearful that God will not be willing to forgive them for the guilt of ending the life of their baby. 1 John 1:9

reminds us that, "If we confess our sins, He is faithful and just and will forgive us our sins and purify us from all unrighteousness." God can unhook the pain of true guilt, so you can move into your best life possible.

Abused women often carry a great deal of false guilt. They are programmed to believe that they are the primary problem in the relationship. This condemning feeling keeps women from believing that they have the right to believe in themselves, and they often feel hopeless about the prospect of being involved in a healthy relationship.

ANGER

Anger is an emotion that is commonly unaccepted in our society, especially for women. However, anger is an emotion found throughout the Word of God, so we know the emotion of anger is not always inappropriate. In the grieving process, anger often shows itself because there is a belief that someone needs to take responsibility for what has happened. Someone needs to be blamed.

Anger in itself is not the problem but rather the inappropriate expressions, behaviors, and thoughts associated with it. When anger responses are not kept in check, it's destructive to you, as well as to others. Unlike guilt, which is primarily destructive to yourself because it's inward, anger is also destructive to others if you don't develop an ability to control it.

 Anger is an indication that some desired goal in your life has been blocked.

So, if you struggle with anger, examine what goals you feel you are not reaching in your life. Once you know what they are, decide if you can go over the blockage, around the blockage, or just build a new road to reach your goal. If you don't recognize these blocked goals then you'll consistently feel like you have no power in your life, which sets you up to feel like a victim to your circumstances. Feeling like a victim keeps you trapped in anger.

I need to add a word of caution here. A primary dilemma about determining desired goals is that they may not always be valid or reasonable. Some goals can be extremely selfish and harmful. These are not the goals I am talking of (I offer a teaching on anger issues through Karis Counselling Services. If you want to know about how to determine what a healthy goal looks like, visit www.mybestlifepossible.com and learn about available workshops).

 You're not a victim. You have the power to choose how you will respond in life.

You may experience anger because you struggle to accept that life isn't fair. You might declare, "It's not fair. Why has this happened to me?" If you determine that your final conclusion must involve a fair outcome, you will be trapped in anger. Unfortunately, not everything in life is determined by our understanding of fairness. It's true; sometimes life experiences don't make sense. Yet this is not a good reason to stay angry.

You might also get angry with yourself. Self-directed anger is a common struggle. You may blame yourself for what happened and feel a strong sense of anger that you did not stop the situation in the first place. Yet, as you examine your self-blame, you might come to the conclusion that there were situations you truly had no power over at that time. Or, you might have to accept that you were still immature in your decision making. Either way, you cannot change the past.

Unfortunately, when you don't deal with anger in a healthy manner, you become a venomous person. You lash out at people. You angrily explode on people, because you're so mad at yourself, you can't contain it.

 There's no benefit in being angry with yourself.

It benefits no one. You have to learn it's okay to let go, forgive others, forgive yourself, and find new boundaries for dealing with anger.

If you're living a life of blame, hatred or anger aimed toward yourself, it's time to get unhooked from it. Discover what goals were blocked and determine what secondary losses you've had (revisit Step 3). Come to know your real feelings. Get unhooked from anger, because if anger isn't taken care of, it becomes extremely destructive and controls you.

How To Own Your Anger

We're each born with predispositions for our personality and character. Some people are born with a more laid back personality while others seem to naturally be more intense. I see anger feelings as being like a stick of dynamite with a wick on the end of it. If you're born with a laid back personality, you have a very long wick on the end of the dynamite stick and it takes many experiences for the anger emotions to reach the explosives. You have more time to evaluate how anger is affecting you. Therefore, you are less likely to get stuck in the anger component of grief.

If you are a person born with a very short wick, you may experience anger feelings regularly. You may often find yourself exploding more readily. The time between the feeling and the reaction is minimal.

You can't lengthen the wick you were given, but you can work through the components of dealing with your anger.

That way, you're more able to stop the fire before it reaches the dynamite.

It's not easy to deal with anger, but you do have the power to change your life, your perspective, and how you deal with the length of your wick. You're not a victim. If you're in the victim mode, you're likely stuck; you feel there's nothing you can do, but that's not true.

my life *Throughout my life, I have struggled with anger and exploded many times without realizing I could actually do something about it. Once I acknowledged that I was born with a shorter wick, I accepted the truth that I am more prone to feelings of anger. This has helped me gain a better hold on my anger outbursts. I accept that I have to be more attentive to my feelings and thoughts so they do not grow into explosive outbursts. I'm passionate about things in life, and how I deal with that characteristic is important. I can teach myself how to respond when experiencing anger, learn to accept my short wick, and then unhook myself so that I'm not exploding. I have the choice and strength to stop myself.*

DEPRESSION

The next component of grief is depression, which is another topic commonly considered taboo. There seems to still be a great deal of shame around this mental health struggle.

 Depression isn't about the person. It's about an illness.

Although you might be ashamed to acknowledge you're struggling with depression, let me remind you that it is common with grief and loss. It's normal to experience a mild degree of depression while going through the active grieving cycle. However, getting stuck in depression is reason for concern.

Let's look at some symptoms of depression. A clinical guideline for determining if you are depressed is to confirm that you are experiencing a number of the following symptoms for two weeks straight or longer.

Physically, you're likely lethargic. You feel drained. You don't have the motivation to do things you used to do.

You might want to sleep away the day, yet sometimes you might have insomnia (you can't sleep at all).

There's a change in your eating patterns. You might not feel hungry, or you overeat.

Mentally, you might think, "Why bother?" as if there's no hope. Your thinking becomes more and more negative until you can't see anything positive in your day. Be very concerned if you are having self-harming thoughts. You should access help right away if this is happening.

Another mental aspect is that you may become forgetful, confused, and indecisive.

Socially, you might begin to avoid going out or being in relationships with others. You might begin to feel you don't fit in with your friends anymore.

Although the spiritual aspect is not evaluated in the mental health criteria, it still is affected. Spiritually, you may begin to feel like God doesn't care about you. You might feel too drained to read your Bible or pray. You might even feel angry that God is allowing you to feel depressed.

Depression is about withdrawing from life. You find yourself losing all motivation to do what you've normally done.

Continue to educate yourself about depression. Talk to your family about how you're feeling. Don't be ashamed if you're struggling with depression. Always see a medical doctor, and also consider going to a counsellor. Talk therapy is very helpful. Depression is an illness that can attack anyone. The key is to not allowing it to take control of your life.

 If you keep your depression a secret, it could grow out of control. Don't get stuck. Ask for help.

HOPE

The last component to grief is hope. Hope doesn't always mean everything is going smoothly, but you can tell you have hope when you can say, "I can face tomorrow. There's a future in my life." You might temporarily lose sight of hope, but you don't get stuck.

Hope is about reframing your life in spite of what loss you have experienced.

A healthy grief cycle will always end with the hope component. Hope is the other side of grief. Although the experience of grief will always impact your life, hope allows you to move past the experience of loss. Moving into hope is about seeing life through a new lens, which includes the loss.

 Hope is not forgetting the loss, but rather living with the loss.

Hope is the component of grief that you should be striving for. It is the motivator for life. It brings purpose again. Always remember, "For I know the plans I have for you," declares the LORD, "plans to prosper you and not to harm you, plans to give you hope and a future" (Jeremiah 29:11).

As you go through the components of grief, you might experience more than one at a time. It's important to be aware of how you're responding to each component and whether or not you're getting stuck in a specific one. Give yourself space to grieve. Acknowledge what you're going through, give it some space, and then choose to let it go and move on.

Prayer

Dear God,

Grieving is hard to do and I know it's something I don't look forward to. Yet I recognize that actively grieving will bring me the freedom I so long for. Give me the courage and strength to work through this process.

In Jesus' name,

Amen.

Digging In

How were you taught to respond to loss?

What past experiences have you told yourself are "no big deal"?

What is the scariest thing about allowing yourself to actively grieve?

What have you been taught in regards to the idea of receiving counselling?

In what stories of your life have you believed false guilt (condemnation)?

Is there any true guilt (conviction) in your life that you still have not confessed to God yet?

What percentage of your day do you spend in anger?

How do you respond in anger?

What goals do you feel are being blocked in your life?

In what ways can you make changes to see your goals unblocked?

Do you have a short wick or a long wick? What can you do to keep the dynamite from exploding?

Which depression symptoms do you experience? Are you seeking medical and emotional support in order to overcome the depression?

What would hope look like for you?

In your own words, write what you've learned from this chapter.

His Words Of Hope

† "Even though I walk through the valley of the shadow of death, I will fear no evil, for you are with me; your rod and your staff, they comfort me. You prepare a table before me in the presence of my enemies. You anoint my head with oil; my cup overflows. Surely your goodness and love will follow me all the days of my life, and I will dwell in the house of the LORD forever" (Psalm 23:4-6).

† "I have swept away your offenses like a cloud, your sins like the morning mist. Return to me, for I have redeemed you" (Isaiah 44:22).

† "Weeping may remain for a night, but rejoicing comes in the morning" (Psalm 30:5b).

† "He heals the brokenhearted and binds up their wounds" (Psalm 147:3).

† I will turn their mourning into gladness; I will give them comfort and joy instead of sorrow" (Jeremiah 31:13b).

Step 5

Challenge Your Beliefs

A belief is the mental acceptance of a claim that something is true (whether or not it is). Beliefs are formed by what you think and experience. As a young child, your primary belief systems are formed by what you are told. As you grow, your beliefs are based on processing what you experience and what you think truth is.

Beliefs define your meaning of life. They establish your core values and determine how you behave.

All your life decisions are filtered through your beliefs. If you randomly believe things without paying attention to the basis of those beliefs, you'll find yourself making decisions in life without knowing why. Discern the difference between the truth and lies of your beliefs, so you can unhook from all beliefs based in lies.

Beliefs shouldn't be ignored, since beliefs direct actions. It's important to know why you do what you do. Once you understand how to identify your beliefs and connect them to your behavior, you can help yourself and others to better understand your actions.

When you have a thought, you make a choice to believe it or not. When you believe something, you act on it. It's important to know the link between your beliefs, thoughts, and actions.

Some of your beliefs are faulty, and some aren't. Even if you've been raised with many solid, valid beliefs, you likely also have faulty beliefs, especially if you've been carrying around the burden of traumatic experiences in life.

 The two most important things are: to know what you believe, <u>and</u> whether the belief is true or false.

WHERE BELIEFS COMES FROM

You were taught some beliefs as you were growing up. Perhaps at home you were taught about manners, respect, and how to live with others in the family. You were taught in school, as well as many other situations. You've also been taught by media and peers. As you've been taught, you've been encouraged to embrace and believe a variety of things.

It's interesting to look at the differences between generations. The beliefs I have might not be taught to the younger generation of today. The differences in beliefs affect how people relate to one another.

It's also important to realize you might feel you no longer want to believe many things you were taught, as some of your beliefs have possibly been built on lies, which results in faulty beliefs. You may be conflicted about letting them go because they seem to be connected to your past experiences and teachings.

 Everything you see and hear is not necessarily true. You don't have to believe everything. You have the right to choose not to believe some things.

In addition to being taught what to believe, you also gain beliefs from what you have experienced, or at least how you have interpreted your experiences. You and I could have the same experience but end up holding a very different belief as a result of that experience. It's the interpretation of that experience that causes us to establish certain beliefs.

Another way you gain beliefs is from your ideals. You have ideals of what you think life should look like in such areas as marriage, family, and career. If ideals are built on faulty thinking or if they don't work out the way you hoped, the beliefs you gather from the ideals will often be unhealthy.

WHY IT IS IMPORTANT TO KNOW YOUR BELIEFS

Your beliefs are deeply rooted in who you are and what you do, even when you don't intentionally think about those connections. It's important to try to figure out the whys of what you're doing and what you're thinking.

my life *When I talk to a woman who shares something she believes, I ask her who (or what experience) taught that belief to her. Many times, she doesn't know, so we begin to look back, searching for the first time she can identify having believed whatever it is. The process helps her learn to find out who taught her, or how she came to learn the belief, which will then help her decide whether it's true or not, and whether she needs to unhook it or not.*

For example, let's assume a belief starts as a result of childhood sexual abuse. You believe you're a shameful person because why else would someone violate you that way? It's a belief you'll hold throughout your life if you don't discover it's not a valid belief. You'll act on the belief, doing shame-based things and having shame-based thoughts, because you believe you're shameful. You only live according to your belief about what you are worth.

You might also feel you are being shamed by others even when they're not trying to shame you, because you have a core belief that you're a shameful woman. It's the same for any kind of traumatic experience. All emotions that come with such an experience, and the interpretations that follow, need to be challenged by you as an adult.

You should go into the past of your story, not to ruminate and get stuck in it, but to learn something from it. As a child, there were many beliefs you didn't necessarily have the ability to challenge. You didn't have the same amount of power in your life as you do as an adult. As an adult, you absolutely have the right to go back and challenge any belief, especially beliefs that are based on lies and aren't healthy.

The next time you catch yourself wondering why you're doing something, think about what you believe about it. Then try to determine where you learned the basis for that belief. Next, determine if you still have to believe the same thing at this time in your life. If it's not the truth, don't continue to believe it. You don't have to keep the same interpretation that you had as a child.

 You have the power to challenge what you believe. It's important to get to the root of things.

Matthew 15:18 says, "But the things that come out of the mouth come from the heart, and these make a man 'unclean'." If you want to know what your beliefs are, listen to what you say (whether you are saying these things out loud or in your mind).

 You need to be careful about what you say to yourself.

If you devalue yourself, you can cause deep harm to your life. When you speak lies to yourself, you're drinking poison. If you drink poison, you'll slowly die, because poison doesn't make people well. Replace the poison with the medicine of God's Word, correcting the damage you've done to yourself.

The next time you want to say something negative to yourself, put yourself down, or devalue yourself, imagine

209

yourself taking that glass of poison and drinking a little bit. Ask, "Am I worth more than this poison?" Yes, you are! Put the poison aside and bring in the medicine.

Remember, your words feed your thinking, and your thinking feeds your words. They go hand in hand. Line up all your thinking and all your words to the truth of God's words, because truth is going to set you free. Truth is what is going to give you the ability to move ahead in life, instead of sabotaging yourself. Truth will help you get unhooked from past experiences. Truth will help you change your interpretation of past experiences. Truth will help you to move forward, forgiving yourself, forgiving others, and determining to learn from your experiences and emotional pain.

 You can't change your story, but you can find freedom from its impact through knowing the truth.

Keep in mind there are many untruths in the world. Many times lies are mixed with a little bit of truth, so you swallow them more easily. You might take one bite and then another and another without discerning what you're thinking until you've accepted many lies.

Remember, there's only one place to get truth: the Word of God. There is no other truth. Truth isn't subjective. It doesn't change with situations. God's truth is solid.

 It's important to know that truth is not a feeling. Truth is fact. It can't change with time or situations like feelings do.

Don't focus your life experiences on how you feel. Your goal in life is to put the truth ahead of feelings, causing your feelings to follow behind the truth. Quiet your feelings, and listen to truth. You don't need to waste time and energy chasing your feelings all over the place.

Claiming truth in your life can be scary and uncomfortable. You might feel as if you're being phony because you don't yet believe the truth deep in your heart. But, if you live by feelings first, you'll dismiss many valuable truths. Truth isn't about feelings. Truth is about facts. Truth sets you free, and lies put you in bondage.

Lies bring confusion, but truth gives clarity, which helps you move forward.

WHY IT IS HARD TO CHANGE BELIEFS

When you live a life in which you believe many lies, you might not even realize what they are. You may hold the following beliefs about yourself:

- I'm not worthy.

- I'm no good.

- I need to be liked by everybody.

- I need to please everybody.

- I must be perfect.

All these statements are lies and aren't from God. These and other lies can appear real to you because they line up with what you tell yourself daily. Yet, they are extreme statements.

 Don't tear yourself apart and say negative things about yourself.

When you use words like must, should, always, and never, you're likely believing a lie to some degree. These words give no freedom for growth, which involves making mistakes, and learning through trial and error. For example, if you've had a rough day at work, you might say, "I never do anything right." That's not true. You do many things right. It is just that you may have erred in one aspect of your job that day. To give that one aspect so much precedent over your overall belief about yourself is crippling and tainting truth in your life.

As you continually hear yourself say such negative things, you'll begin to accept them as truth. You'll begin to spiral downward, becoming depressed and worrisome with whatever comes to mind.

Perhaps you go home and respond similarly to your family. You say, "I never do it right." Never is extreme, and it's very seldom an accurate perception. Take out the word "never". Instead say, "I didn't do it right today." That is a more accurate statement. It's the truth for today but not necessarily for tomorrow.

Another phrase to avoid using is "I can't." "I can't" is a victim statement. When you replace it with "I won't," you're being truthful. You set yourself free to make decisions based on what you will or will not do.

 Little words can be powerful and can hold you back from living an unhooked life.

You might believe that God can never forgive you for some things you have done. You intellectually know that the Bible assures you that He forgives. However, you might still decide that He can forgive everything else except that one thing you did. That is a lie of the devil. That's what the devil wants you to believe because it will keep you stuck. In order to combat lies, you must find truth.

 For every lie Satan throws at you there is a truth in Scripture to combat it.

For example, 1 John 1:9 says, "If we confess our sins, He is faithful and just and will forgive us our sins and purify us from all unrighteousness." This means all, with no exceptions. Know the Bible so you can know the truth!

214

It's challenging to discern truth from lies. You become familiar with the way you're living, so it's foreign to examine how you think. It takes work to replace lies with truth. It can be emotionally draining, but if you stick with it and don't give up, you'll become familiar with truth, and lies will become foreign. Right now you are in a cycle of believing lies. That is what is holding you back.

 The lies seem so familiar that you might not even recognize them.

Be encouraged. As you begin to develop a new way of thinking, you will find and put truth into your life.

WHERE TO LOOK FOR TRUTH

The first place to look for truth is the Word of God. You can always believe it. Study it, memorize scriptures, and use it as your blueprint for life.

Another place to gain truth is to attend a Bible-believing church. Make friends, get involved, listen to sermons, and participate in Bible studies. Surround yourself with people who will tell you the truth. Don't spend the majority of your time with people who believe lies or don't want to find truth.

When you're changing your patterns of thinking, you're not just redoing the patterns you're in; you're starting new patterns. You're feeding new beliefs. It takes a lot of time and effort to build a new system, and you need support along the way. Afterall, it took a lot of time to develop the patterns you have now, too. So be determined that you can change. Don't be satisfied with falling back into your old patterns of doing things. Move forward and get unhooked.

 It's not any easier to live in a lie than it is to live in the truth.

Always keep in mind the two ways you can deal with emotional pain. When you decide to start going through your emotional pain, instead of moving around it, you might imagine it's harder work because you're challenging your thinking all the time. Yes, challenging your thoughts and beliefs takes effort but it does not take any more effort than it does to live in the lie. Believing there's an easy route is just another lie.

Since everything you do will not be easy as you change your beliefs and build a new pattern in your life be sure to take a short break now and then. You don't have to be doing emotional work 24/7. You can have an occasional break. Make sure you take care of yourself, do some things you like to do, and stay involved. Take a break, but don't quit. Building a new pattern happens one small step after another.

Also, remember that what you feed grows, and what you starve dies. Lies are easily fed. You might not recognize how much they're growing. When you catch yourself believing a lie, you don't need to punish yourself. Just take that opportunity to change the thought. When you punish yourself, you can easily spiral downward into a place where you feel less valued and less hopeful.

A simple question you can ask yourself is, "If I feed this thought, what will it grow into?" Or, "If I starve this thought, what will die?" Your challenge is to actually starve the negative and feed the positive.

Be patient. You'll get tired and want to give up. Imagine having a plant you want to grow. It doesn't grow overnight. You have to consistently water it. You have to reliably care for it. The outcome is a beautiful, vibrant plant.

It's the same for feeding truth and starving lies that come into your mind. I promise you that over time, if you put these principles into practice, you will mature and grow in your life. If you go through your emotional pain, seeking truth and building new patterns, forcing out the lies, you'll live with hope, joy, and peace.

Prayer

Dear God,

I know I hold a lot of beliefs in my heart. Help me to be aware of which beliefs to challenge, which to change, and which to keep.

In Jesus' name,

Amen.

Digging In

What are your core values and beliefs?

How often do you examine your behaviors alongside your beliefs?

What childhood beliefs do you need to challenge?

On a scale of 1 – 10 (10 being 100%), how much do you believe you have the right to challenge your beliefs, especially if they were taught to you by someone in authority?

What does your ideal life look like?

To what degree are you living your ideal life?

What faulty beliefs are holding you back from living your ideal life now?

What words or statements do you use to devalue yourself in your self-talk?

How often do you study the Word of God so you are able to discern truth from lies?

Do you primarily live by feelings or by truth?

In your own words, write what you've learned from this chapter.

Words Of Hope

✝ "If any of you lacks wisdom, he should ask God, who gives generously to all without finding fault, and it will be given to him" (James 1:5).

✝ "Be self-controlled and alert. Your enemy the devil prowls around like a roaring lion looking for someone to devour" (1 Peter 5:8).

✝ "So I say, live by the Spirit, and you will not gratify the desires of the sinful nature" (Galatians 5:16).

✝ "Since, then, you have been raised with Christ, set your hearts on things above, where Christ is seated at the right hand of God. Set your minds on things above, not on earthly things. For you died, and your life is now hidden with Christ in God" (Colossians 3:1-3).

✝ "We demolish arguments and every pretension that sets itself up against the knowledge of God, and we take captive every thought to make it obedient to Christ" (2 Corinthians 10:5).

Step 6

Choose To Forgive

Forgiveness is a spiritual act. It makes no sense in the natural, because there seems to be no justice in forgiveness. However, it's something God tells us to do. Choosing to forgive is one of the foundational steps a person must take in order to see a turn-around in their life.

my life — *I can honestly say that the most profound changes I see in any woman happens when she decides to forgive from her heart. It is like there is a new spirit about her. I see it on her face. I see it in her eyes. I hear it in her voice. I recognize it from her words. Once she has stepped out of unforgivenss her healing speeds up termendously. It is incredible how the act of forgivenss transforms a person.*

Even though it seems unnatural to forgive someone who has harmed you, you can follow through with God's plan and forgive. God shares the importance of forgiving in His Word. Colossians 3:13 says, "Bear with each other and forgive whatever grievances you may have against one another. Forgive as the Lord forgave you." In Ephesians 4:32 it reads, "Be kind and compassionate to one another, forgiving each other, just as in Christ God forgave you."

 When you forgive you are saying that the guilt resulting from the wrongdoing is pardoned.

Keep in mind these principles surrounding forgiveness aren't just about deep traumas that have happened in your life. These principles can be used in all areas of hurt in your life – large and small.

THE IMPORTANCE OF FORGIVENESS

First, God is in the business of reconciliation. He reconciled people to Himself. That is why Jesus came into the world. He is the way to reconciliation with God.

Also, God knows unforgiveness destroys unity, hope, and love for people. Unforgiveness can cause terrible turmoil and pain in a person's life, and that's not part of God's plan.

Jesus also stresses that the importance of forgiveness is vital to your relationship with Him. He says in Matthew 6:14-15, "For if you forgive men when they sin against you, your heavenly Father will also forgive you. But if you do not forgive men their sins, your Father will not forgive your sins." That is a sobering statement to consider.

Jesus modelled forgiveness for you, so you can trust forgiveness as the correct road. You can know it's true and right. You can trust forgiveness as the good answer to your struggles. Forgiveness is possible because God has said it's possible.

WHAT UNFORGIVENESS LOOKS LIKE

Unforgiveness is an illegitimate response to a legitimate need.

The legitimate desire is to have a painful experience made right. Yet, the illegitimate response to a painful experience is unforgiveness.

Unforgiveness expresses itself in many ways. One way is in a bitter spirit, which often shows on your face and in your voice. Hebrews 12:15 says, "See to it that no one misses the grace of God and that no bitter root grows up to cause trouble and defile many." Roots are necessary for growth. In unforgiveness, a root of bitterness takes hold in your heart.

Roots aren't detectable by the naked eye. You don't realize how strong and deep and wide a root is until you're ready to remove it from the ground.

Have you ever tried to uproot a plant only to discover that the root is way bigger and deeper than you thought? It takes way more time and effort to remove than you ever expected.

The same thing happens with bitterness. You have to be on guard because bitterness grows undetected. When you finally come to a point in your life and recognize you hold bitterness, it's more difficult and painful to remove.

Bitterness To Hate

 If the root of bitterness hasn't been detected, over time, it develops into hate.

You can hate people passively or aggressively. To passively hate someone is to be hardened towards them, finding it difficult to wish them well. Aggressive hate is even harsher than that. It is wishing someone ill. You want someone to be harmed or to experience hurt. You want revenge. If you recognize the signs of aggressive hate in your life, you have a deep root of bitterness in your heart, and it's time to deal with it.

WHY WE STRUGGLE WITH FORGIVENESS

There are many reasons that can hold you back from forgiving. If you're struggling with any of the following reasons, ask God to help you let go.

You Feel Emotional Pain

 It's important to know that the act of forgiveness itself doesn't always immediately minimize the pain you feel from what happened.

Often the painful aspect of your story takes time to decrease and disappear. You need to continually practice the act of forgiveness throughout this time frame because your heart is seeding and growing forgiveness. And that takes time.

There Seems To Be No Justice In Forgiveness

You might believe that by extending forgiveness the offender will not have to take responsibility for his actions. It may look to be true. There are many things people do that seem to go unpunished in this world. It seems there is no self-responsibility and justice. However, we are all responsible before God. He knows exactly what has happened in your life and in the person's life who offended you.

 Forgiveness is not about your justice. It's about your freedom.

It doesn't matter how small or great the offense was. If you're holding onto it, you're not free. Seek forgiveness, not justice, and let God take care of that aspect.

God has promised He is the one who will avenge us. He has also promised we're only responsible for our own actions. If you choose to forgive someone who has offended you and you don't think he's experienced the punishment or justice that is deserved, trust God. He is aware. He knows what is going on. Reach out and trust Him to give you peace. God is bigger and greater than you.

You're Waiting For Someone To Be Sorry

You might struggle with forgiving because you're waiting for that person to be sorry before you extend forgiveness.

You want him to sincerely apologize to you for what he did.

You're not responsible for someone else's attitude, only your own. You cannot make someone be sorry. You can only choose to forgive someone. It's important to recognize you have power over your own attitude, not someone else's.

 Don't let others take power away from you by letting your forgiveness depend on their regret.

If you decide that your healing is directly based on someone else's decision to be repentant, you could potentially be stuck for a lifetime. Depending on someone else is a heavy burden to put on yourself.

Perhaps the person who offended you is dead. That person will not be able to come to you and say he is sorry. Or, if the person is alive and walking around as if nothing has happened, you still need to recognize that you cannot demand the person come to you to ask you for forgiveness. Be careful that you are not stuck in pain forever. Let yourself off the hook.

Forgiveness is not specifically for the other person. It's for you. It frees you so you can get on with your life.

Don't allow your forgiveness to be hinged on someone else. It would be heartbreaking to live the rest of your life in bitterness, hate, and revenge.

The Offense Doesn't Make Sense

Perhaps you've chosen not to forgive because you believe the wrong that was done to you makes no sense. It likely doesn't, because it is based on someone's sinful behavior.

 If your forgiveness depends on someone else's motives or reasons, you'll feel powerless. You're not responsible for someone else's motive.

The reality is that if you look at patterns in your own life, you might be surprised to find that you have also behaved in senseless offensive ways to others at one time or another.

Every one of us has harmed someone else in some way. We all have the potential to harm. It's important to recognize your potential to offend, especially as you consider your forgiveness of someone who has hurt you. Recognize your own heart. Although your offense may not be as great as someone who offended you, it is still an offense.

 Jesus did not say you forgive according to the level of the offense. He says forgive. Period.

Matthew 6:14-15 says, "For if you forgive men when they sin against you, your heavenly Father will also forgive you. But if you do not forgive men their sins, your Father will not forgive your sins." Now that's heavy. Jesus says that forgiveness for your actions towards others is only to the extent that you are willing to forgive someone else.

Forgiveness is more difficult if we focus all our hopes on people. Instead we need to focus our hope on Jesus.

 Keep your eyes on Jesus, not on humanity.

Keeping your eyes on humanity can often lead to feelings of failure, disgust towards others, and disappointment.

We will all be disappointed by other people, and all of us occasionally disappoint others. Don't keep your eyes on people. People will mess up your perspective. Focus on God. Walk through the pain.

my life *When I was a fairly new Christian, I was dating someone who seemed to be a great Christian guy. I thought the relationship was just what I was looking for. However, the person tried some inappropriate sexual actions towards me. I was appalled and started thinking all Christian men were terrible and couldn't be trusted. I became very bitter.*

This person played the drums in church. I would go to church, and as he'd be playing the drums, I'd start to get very angry inside. I disliked him so much that sometimes I felt like my skin was crawling. I couldn't stand listening to those drums. It infuriated me that the guy who was playing the drums in church wasn't who he claimed to be. It was terrible. I started hating him, even hoping something terrible would happen to him.

I talked to my pastor and shared everything with him. Pastor Peter Cuke was so gentle and said, "Karen, I heard everything you said, and you need to forgive him."

"Forgive him? Are you kidding? Look at what he did to me!"

233

"Karen, you've got to choose to forgive him. It's for your freedom. Don't look to people. Look to Jesus. Look at the answers He has for you, and you'll grow." He continued, "And once you choose to forgive, whenever the feelings of bitterness and anger come back up, just keep reminding yourself that you've already chosen to forgive."

I learned to begin forgiving. It wasn't easy. I made the commitment to forgive, but for a long time, whenever I heard the drums, or saw this guy, feelings of bitterness would begin to rise. I'd pull them out by the roots every time and declare, "No. I chose to forgive."

I looked to God and realized I couldn't focus on people. I couldn't look to people for my answers to the problems in my life, and I couldn't look to people to not let me down. They will let me down at times. God won't.

Over time, I got to a point where I could remember the story of what had happened to me and not have the pain. I even began praying for this person versus praying against him. And the bonus is that I began to love the sound of the drums again!

You Feel Like It's Too Hard

 Forgiveness is not a feeling. Forgiveness is a choice.

If forgiveness was a feeling, Christ would have never died on the cross for us. His crucifixion was all for our forgiveness. Yet, in the garden of Gethsemane He prayed, "My Father, if it is possible, may this cup be taken from me. Yet not as I will, but as you will" (Matthew 26:39b). Jesus was not enjoying the idea of this decision. He did it by choice. He is your example. You need to put your feelings behind the outcome of the act of forgiveness. God wants you to be free from bitterness and hate. Yes, it is hard, but not impossible.

You Think Forgiving Always Must Equal Forgetting

God gave you the ability to remember. Just because you forgive, it does not automatically mean you will forget the incidence that caused you pain. Even when you forgive, you won't forget every detail of what happened.

The problem is that unforgiveness is like a huge rope around your waist, and wherever you go, you're hauling

235

along a heavy burden. Yet as you forgive, you can take this rope and turn it into a thread. You can change the weight of the rope. You may never fully forget your experience, but healing isn't about forgetting.

 Healing is about remembering and being free in spite of it.

Although the truth of the story goes with you wherever you go, you can take ownership of its impact so it doesn't have so much power in your life. A thread is much lighter to carry than a heavy rope!

You may think you have the strength to carry the heavy rope, but it weighs you down. You get depressed, discouraged, and hopeless. That is why you need to forgive. Your threads might be sewn to horrific past stories but you no longer need to be burdened the same.

To have a memory of something negative is not the same as harboring and feeding a grudge. Painful feelings may still come up, but as you choose to forgive, the pain will become less and less. You won't harbor a grudge. You will experience the freedom that God intends. Imagine how that will feel for you!

You Think Forgiveness Always Equals Reconciliation

If you forgive, do you have to be in relationship with that person again? This is a very sensitive question to respond to. It can be frightful to think that as you forgive an abuser that you are required to be back in relationship with him again.

Although you must respect all people as created in the image of God, because they're valuable before God, forgiveness doesn't alter the truth that sometimes a person may not be healthy for you. Although reconciliation is God's example to us it may not always happen. You can't keep people in your life if they are making the relationship unhealthy.

Since reconciliation is a two-way street – some will choose not to be reconciled and your hands are tied in regards to that relationship.

Plus, sometimes past actions do reap heavy consequences. There was a time when Paul and Barnabas parted ways

(Acts 15:39). There is also a good example in the Bible of David being in harms way and having to find protection from Saul on more than one occasion(I Samuel).

Not everyone is ready to be in a healthy relationship with someone else. Unfortunately, there are those individuals who can be physically, emotionally, mentally, or spiritually abusive. The healthier you get, the less willing you'll be to let unhealthy people into your life. Your value (or theirs) doesn't change, but their lifestyle situation might have to change before you can be in relationship with them again.

Give yourself permission to lead a healthy life, because you're free. If you allow someone unhealthy into your life, their unhealthiness will begin to seep into you (Visit www.mybestlifepossible.com for teaching on boundary-setting).

Letting Go Seems Scary

If you forgive someone, you will have to stop living as a victim. If you stop living like a victim, you must take ownership of your life and make healthy decisions. That in itself can cause fear and dread. Sometimes it seems easier to continue living like a victim, because you then have someone to blame for your miserable situation. That's not freedom. Owning your life is the freedom.

You Might Have To Give Up Being Right

Sometimes when we forgive, we have to give up the right of being correct about the situation. Most of us like to be right. However, being right isn't as important as being unhooked. Pain, bitterness, and hate isn't worth it. Being right isn't as important as your own freedom.

The Person Will Only Do It Again

Yes, they just might. Peter was concerned about that exact issue. Matthew 18: 21-22 says, "Then Peter came to Jesus and asked, "Lord, how many times should I forgive my brother when he sins against me? Up to seven times?" Jesus answered, "I tell you not seven times, but seventy times seven."

Does that sound a bit unrealistic to you? After all, why should that person receive any type of grace from you? Let me ask you this. What if God numbered the times He is willing to forgive you? Would your number be up by now?

I've Tried, And It Didn't Work

All your negative feelings will continue trying to rise up. Feelings will keep coming up with the stories. You're going to have to challenge them every time and reclaim forgiveness. As you repeat it over and over, you're feeding truth. Lies will starve. You'll experience freedom.

 As you confess forgiveness, the act of forgiveness is instant, but it often takes time to come to grips in your heart.

Hang in there. If you have a deep-rooted pain or hurt in your life, don't give up easily, saying, "Well, I tried to forgive him, but it didn't work."

Remember, you're battling memories. You're reworking beliefs. Acknowledge your pain and walk through it, not around it. Don't get stuck ruminating, discussing, and feeding the hurt. Decide you're going to forgive that person.

 Remember the cross. If Jesus can, by choice, die on a cross for your forgiveness, then you can, by choice, die to your belief that you can't forgive.

You Don't Feel Like Forgiving

Perhaps you think, "If I forgive, I'll be a hypocrite, because I don't want to. I don't feel like it." Obedience to God's Word is not hypocrisy. No matter what God asks you to do through His Word, you should follow it regardless of what you feel. This is an example of how truth should overrule your feelings. It's a choice. Be obedient. Obedience leads to freedom.

Forgiveness Of Self

We've worked through many reasons you may find it difficult or refuse to forgive others. What if you are the offender though? It's often even more challenging to accept that you can be forgiven. If you confess your shortcomings to the Lord, you are forgiven! Yet you may struggle to embrace God's grace because ultimately you know your heart and motives better than anyone. If you struggle with this, remember that God does not keep records like you do. Although you may have the memories of your errors and mistakes, God has no reminder of it if you have gone to Him with a repentant heart. Accept His grace. It cost Him everything.

Are you at a crossroads and you need to let go? Do you need to forgive somebody for something? Maybe it's even yourself. Move beyond the crossroads. Make a decision that leads to the best life possible.

 Forgiveness will steer the course of your life in a new, healthy direction.

Prayer

Dear God,

You know how I struggle to let some things go in my heart. You know I have numerous excuses for not forgiving. I recognize that none of them are valid. Help me to truly forgive and accept forgiveness, so I can live in the freedom You offer me.

In Jesus' name,

Amen.

Digging In

How is forgiveness practiced in your life?

Was forgiveness practiced when you were a child?

What crossroads are you at right now? What does the end of each road look like?

What seeds of bitterness have you planted in your heart?

Do you sometimes experience hate in your heart?

To whom are you passively hateful?

To whom are you aggressively hateful?

What would it feel like to be free from anger, hate, and bitterness?

Which of the suggestions for why someone does not forgive are you using?

Is there someone you need to forgive right now? If so, what is stopping you?

In your own words, write what you've learned from this chapter.

His Words Of Hope

† "If we confess our sins, he is faithful and just and will forgive us our sins and purify us from all unrighteousness" (1 John 1:9).

† "I sought the LORD, and he answered me; he delivered me from all my fears. Those who look to him are radiant; their faces are never covered with shame" (Psalm 34:4-5).

† "'No one, sir,' she said. 'Then neither do I condemn you,' Jesus declared. 'Go now and leave your life of sin'" (John 8:11).

† "He who conceals his sins does not prosper, but whoever confesses and renounces them finds mercy" (Proverbs 28:13).

† "When they hurled their insults at him, he did not retaliate; when he suffered, he made no threats. Instead, he entrusted himself to him who judges justly" (1 Peter 2:23).

Step 7

Let Go And Live In Today

Can you believe we're on Step 7 already? Good for you for working hard to get free from the pain of past experiences you've been hanging on to! You're basing your decisions and steps on God's truth and His promise of freedom and hope for your life. You can trust God. Even when the steps He guides you through aren't easy, you can know you'll be safe as you obey what He teaches you.

It's not easy to walk through pain, but it's profitable. In the end, you will have ownership of your life.

Even as you're letting go and living in today, it can be easy to get pulled back into your old way of thinking. The old way of thinking is like going back into familiar territory. It is like going back to your natural habitat. Sometimes you'll see that you've moved ahead, but then you can find yourself right back where you were, feeling you haven't moved on at all.

Let's determine some strategies to help you keep on track to live in today so you don't get pulled back into your old way of thinking.

Be patient with yourself. The unhooking process doesn't happen overnight.

It takes time. Life is a journey, and time isn't something you should get angry or agitated about, because life takes time. Instead of fighting it, let time be your friend. Time is what gives you the option to grow.

 Do not measure yourself against perfection. Instead, measure yourself by your movement towards a healthy lifestyle.

You might slip a little backwards once in a while, but with plans and strategies, you're likely to get out of that backward movement more quickly. Celebrate your successes. Yes, you took a step back, but did you stay there as long this time? Did you realize sooner that you slipped? Did you do something different this time so you weren't impacted the same way? Were you less paralyzed? Good for you!

The goal isn't perfection. The goal is freedom from the impact of stuff that's holding you back. It is about finding positive movement in your life. You will get unhooked and live in the today!

WHY YOU SHOULD LET GO

Letting Go Brings Freedom

Freedom doesn't mean you'll have no more problems in life. Freedom means that when problems come, you don't get as tripped up on them because of old patterns. Freedom means you don't get pulled back, held down, and hung up.

my life

I now live a freer life, but I didn't always. I used to get paralyzed very easily by specific things in my life. The pain would be excruciating, and I would spiral downward. Even though there are still moments I get a little caught, I don't spiral anymore. I don't get paralyzed anymore. Some days it's a little harder to experience freedom than others, but the majority of the time, I live in freedom.

My freedom first came from knowing the truth of who I am in God. He made me a valuable human being, and I learned I didn't have to allow my life experiences or my character to own me. My life growth stuff doesn't equal my value.

Whenever past pain or stories try to pull me back, I remind myself that I do not have to stay there. I literally say to myself, "Karen, take owenership of your day. God has a better plan for your day. Decide to walk in it because you've already let go."

Letting Go Gives You Ownership

No other person owns your life. Let go of the past, and own your life today. Give yourself permission to take responsibility for your day.

It's awful to live like a puppet because of your past. It's like you're being pulled in every direction by strings that take away your input or control. When you let go, you cut the strings. You're not moved around by feelings, fears, and doubts.

You have ownership of your life. God gave each of us individual lives. He wants you to own your life and live it to the fullest, being used and blessed by Him. In the process, you will also bless other people.

Letting Go Allows You To Be Productive

my life *Have you ever had one of those non-productive days? I used to have a lot of unproductive days. Because my focus was in the past, and I was filled with fear and I couldn't be productive in my today. Nothing seemed to get settled in*

251

my world. I'd look back at the end of the day and feel so gulity that I did not accomplish my daily tasks and plans I wanted to see done. It's was a difficult way to live.

When you let go, you begin to see productivity in your life. Productivity isn't necessarily only your "to do" list. It's being productive in your heart, productive in your relationships, and productive in some of the plans you have for the day.

 When you let go, you can be productive, because there is nothing holding you back.

HOW TO LET GO AND LIVE IN TODAY

Practice The 7 Steps

Practice, practice, and practice the steps of the *Unhooked!* principles. You might need to practice one step more than others. We're all different. It's okay. Just keep doing it, because you need all the steps in order to live fully in today. Until you've completed the steps, you're still living in your painful experiences.

As you become familiar with the truth and the *Unhooked!* steps, healthy thinking becomes what's familiar to you, and in the process, the hooked unhealthy feelings become unfamiliar. Remember, letting go isn't as easy as just snapping your fingers.

 You have to learn to walk *out* of the unhealthy familiar and walk *into* the healthy unfamiliar, so that eventually the unfamiliar *becomes* your familiar.

Don't Give Up

Following these principles is hard at first, because you're not familiar with the *Unhooked!* strategies. The process might seem tiresome. You might feel weary. Just remind yourself that you are building new patterns in your life, and you're replacing old ones. That takes energy.

It's a challenge to not get caught up in living in the past or only focusing on the future. When you haven't unhooked from your past, you can get consumed with feelings of hopelessness.

Remember that you have to commit to your today, in order to change tomorrow.

Use Encouragement

Instead of asking yourself, "When will this change?", you need to say, "Today I will make the change; right now." It's helpful to feed your mind with daily words of encouragement. Put words of encouragement around your home, on your computer, in the car, and on your cell phone. Encouragement helps you live in today. It helps you stop and smell the flowers.

Encouraging words seed reminders of hope.

Plan

Plan to let go and live in today, so you won't be waiting for the wind to blow you here and there. Perhaps you've said, "Where did the day go? It was kind of a waste. I don't feel like I even lived today as my mind was somewhere else."

You might need to start small, taking ownership by planning an hour at a time. You might need a day planner or another organizational tool to force you out of your pain and focus on today. If you don't plan to intercept your thoughts, feelings, and actions, you'll find that time goes by quickly. Before you know it, another week or month has passed.

Living in today helps you be more intentional versus aimless. You'll feel less scattered because you have a plan. It is purposeful living.

 When you're living in today, you are a decision maker. You're intentional.

When you live in today, you're in control of your decisions instead of feeling as if decisions are in control of you. Jot down a plan, and make it happen.

Be Aware And Catch Yourself

Another way to live in today is to catch yourself when you're thinking and dwelling on things. Be attentive to your thinking patterns throughout your day. When you live in today, you're more emotionally aware of your life, because you're more in tune with what you're doing, thinking, and feeling. It's hard work at first, but it provides you with a sense of being alive.

It is so easy to just let your mind wander. As you go over and over the same stories in your mind you can become paralyzed with sadness, fear and anger. Here's a tip: if what you are thinking on in regards to your past is not for a specific healing and growth exercise, then challenge yourself to focus your mind on the task at hand. Don't allow your mind to drift. It is not productive to let your thoughts drag you away from your purpose at hand.

Once you catch your thinking pattern, make a decision to redirect it. Decide if the things you are thinking on are valuable for your growth at the time. Of course, if there's something truthful and usable you can learn from the past, bring it into today as a source of support for the new patterns you are building.

my life *I help women learn to go back, examine their beliefs, and name their losses. I'm not asking people to settle into their pasts so they fall apart, get stuck, and feel like victims again. I'm asking them to temporarily go to their pasts* *only to see what they can learn. Other than that, there is no reason to allow their mind to dwell.*

One other thought to consider. You also need to catch yourself when you're living in the future mindset. We all have dreams and expectations, which help bring hope for the future. However, when you focus so much on the "I wish, wish, wish" of your life, you can become unsettled with your life and have no peace in your heart. You then live in a fantasy in your mind, which also steals your today.

Build Relationships

Living in today builds relationships. Many women are lonely and don't have a core group of friends. In order to build relationships, you have to invest and live in today. When you live in the past or future, you say such things as, "I remember when I had that great friend," or "Maybe someday I'll be a part of something and have great friends." If you live in today, you'll build relationships now. Step out and become a friend to someone.

Build Memories

Living in today builds memories for tomorrow. Memories sustain you. On rough days, you can say, "Yeah, I remember I lived through this or accomplished that." Make a decision to invest in your life so you have something positive to recall.

Living in today is about taking control of your mind, thoughts, and behaviors. Everything filters through the brain, so you need to have control of the thoughts that flow through it. You can take ownership of living in today, going to the past only to learn something, and moving into the future with the knowledge you built your future by living in the now.

 What you live today will determine your future, and will be your past story.

Prayer

Dear God,

Help me to live in the here and now. The only reason I need to go into the past is to learn how to make my present better. Thank you that I have hope.

In Jesus' name,

Amen

Digging In

Examine how many days out of the week you live in the past or future. What is happening those days that are different from the days you are living in the "now"?

What do you need to do in order to plan your life?

What old patterns do you need to replace?

How do you celebrate your successes?

Change takes time. What reminders can you put in your life to encourage yourself on the rough days?

Do you see time as your enemy?

How can you start measuring your growth by movement, instead of perfection?

Are you actively building relationships and memories?

One a scale of 1-10 (10 = 100%), how much do you trust that God has your best interests in mind?

In your own words, write what you've learned from this chapter.

His Words Of Hope

✝ "But seek first his kingdom and his righteousness, and all these things will be given to you as well. Therefore do not worry about tomorrow, for tomorrow will worry about itself. Each day has enough trouble of its own" (Matthew 6:33-34).

✝ "Do not be anxious about anything, but in everything, by prayer and petition, with thanksgiving, present your requests to God. And the peace of God, which transcends all understanding, will guard your hearts and your minds in Christ Jesus" (Philippians 4:6-7).

✝ "Cast all your anxiety on him because he cares for you" (1 Peter 5:7).

✝ "Brothers, I do not consider myself yet to have taken hold of it. But one thing I do: Forgetting what is behind and straining toward what is ahead, I press on toward the goal to win the prize for which God has called me heavenward in Christ Jesus" (Philippians 3:13-14).

Step 1: Acknowledge Past Experience

Step 2: Recognize And Feel Feelings

Step 3: Name The Loss

Step 4: Understand The Grief Cycle

Step 5: Challenge Your Beliefs

Step 6: Choose To Forgive

Step 7: Let Go And Live In Today

So, What Now?

Wow, you have made it through all 7 steps! You have made a life-changing decision. I am very proud of your willingness to keep going.

Step 1 encouraged you to walk out of the denial and then tell your story. Have you decided how you will move forward? Have you confirmed who you are going to trust?

Step 2 taught you there are more than happy, glad, mad, and sad feelings. It also stressed that emotions are not the real problem. What you do with them is. Have you begun to recognize the deeper feelings, and learned to sit in the uncomfortable ones for a while?

Step 3 encouraged you to dig deeper than your primary loss. In this step, you were able to take ownership of your hooks. It is in this step that you came to know yourself more intimately.

Step 4 gave you a greater understanding of the normal grieving process through loss. It is here that you may have learned you were stuck in one of the components of grief.

Step 5 helped you see there is a need to know truth. It is in this step you learned you have permission to say "no" to lies.

Step 6 challenged you to soften your heart. It is in this step you had the opportunity to truly experience the grace of God as you let go of numerous hurts and resentments.

Step 7 described how you can anchor your life in today while using your past to learn about yourself. This step taught that your "here and now" is truly your future as you practice living your best life possible.

Overall, I know the steps have been challenging, draining, freeing, and enlightening. I encourage you to be patient with your continued healing. I often hear women say they feel tired from the process and don't want to continue to walk through it at times. Getting unhooked is going to take time. Don't be disappointed with yourself. If you continue to challenge yourself and work hard, you can become a new woman. You can be free for the rest of your life.

my life *Years ago, I was a mess. I couldn't do any of these steps. I couldn't imagine I had value, let alone believe I'm a 10/10. I didn't know my worth wasn't based on my character or life experiences. I didn't know my worth was determined by God, who created me in His image.*

I lived in misery, and I believed many lies. I didn't allow myself to move forward in the things of God because I thought God wouldn't use me. I thought I was a terrible person who had many terrible things happen to me. Why would God want to use a woman like me?

But now I am living proof that anyone, including you, can be free, unhooked from your emotional pain and experiences. There is hope. You're not alone even if it feels like that sometimes.

I know there will be times when you think things are not changing, but they are if you are putting the *Unhooked!* steps into practice. Do not weary of doing the hard work.

Feel free to contact me by email at kariscounsel@gmail.com about anything you would like to share concerning your experience as you work through these 7 steps. I am always grateful for your feedback. It is exciting to hear how God uses this book to change lives.

"Forget the former things; do not dwell on the past. See, I am doing a new thing! Now it springs up; do you not perceive it? I am making a way in the desert and streams in the wasteland" (Isaiah 43:18-19).

NOW GO AND LIVE YOUR BEST LIFE POSSIBLE!

Prayer

Dear God,

Thank you for caring enough about me to bring this teaching into my life. Give me the courage to put into practice Your principles for my life so I can live the best life possible. I love you so much.

In Jesus' name,

Amen

Digging In

On a scale of 1-10 (10 being 100%), how much do you believe you have been unhooked?

Which of the 7 steps did you find the hardest to walk through? Why?

Write a description of what it is like for you to be unhooked from your story now. Remind yourself of this description on a daily basis.

In your own words, write what you've learned from this chapter.

His Words Of Hope

✝ "This is how God showed his love among us: He sent his one and only Son into the world that we might live through him" (1 John 4:9).

✝ "Therefore, I urge you, brothers, in view of God's mercy, to offer your bodies as living sacrifices, holy and pleasing to God - this is your spiritual act of worship. Do not conform any longer to the pattern of this world, but be transformed by the renewing of your mind. Then you will be able to test and approve what God's will is - his good, pleasing and perfect will" (Romans 12:1-2).

✝ "The tongue has the power of life and death, and those who love it will eat its fruit" (Proverbs 18:21).

✝ "Let us not become weary in doing good, for at the proper time we will reap a harvest if we do not give up" (Galatians 6:9).

Spiritual Help

God cares about everything you do and everything you've been through. He understands that life has its share of pain and loss. Yet of even greater concern to God is your eternal destination. Jesus said, "What good is it for a man to gain the whole world, and yet lose or forfeit his very self?" (Luke 9:25).

 In other words, there's more to a person than what meets the eye.

God offers you HOPE for your life today and your life after this time on earth. In my opinion there is nothing more needed in a person's life than HOPE. We all need to overflow with it. Hope motivates. Hope keeps a person from despair. Hope offers excitement for something new in life. And hope gives a peace that nothing else can.

my life

I rest my hope in the fact that God is not a liar and He has promised us life in Him, for heaven (eternity) and also for this journey on the earth.

I personally know the difference between life without God (being hopeless) and life with God (being hopeful). Before God, I looked for hope in all the temporal aspects of life…thinking it came from money, power, sex, prestige, and partying. I had a deep searching for some kind of meaning to life. I never quite found it.

When life crashed I realized that none of those things could secure any hope for me.

But then I met God.

I finally came to realize that life on my own was not working. I needed someone to care about me. Everything I believed about life changed when I accepted God into my life. I finally experienced hope.

I want to share with you about the promises HOPE in God gives you. I will use the acronym H.O.P.E.

H is for help. Sometimes life can be tough. Being hopeless in the midst of the daily ups and downs makes it even tougher. God offers you the ultimate help. He answers needs in ways you cannot understand at times. He hears your cry of desperation. He is your complete source of help.

God helps to see that your needs are met: In Matt 6:31-33 Jesus encourages us by saying, "So do not worry, saying "What shall we eat?" or "What shall we drink?" or "What shall we wear?" For the pagans run after all these things, and your heavenly Father knows that you need them. But seek first his kingdom and his righteousness, and all these things will be given to you as well."

God helps you by giving you wisdom and direction: James 1:5 says, "If any of you lacks wisdom, he should ask God, who gives generously to all without finding fault, and it will be given to him."

God promises to strengthen you: Isaiah 41:10 states, "So do not fear, for I am with you; do not be dismayed, for I am your God. I will strengthen you and help you; I will uphold you with my righteous right hand."

God also helps you in your trials: Isaiah 43:2 says, "When you pass through the waters I will be with you, and when you pass through the rivers, they will not sweep over you. When you walk through the fire you will not be burned; the flames will not set you ablaze."

Not only does God help you, He also wants you to express your love for Him by helping others. Which leads me to the O in hope.

O stands for opportunity. God opens doors of opportunity for you to be used by Him. He has gifted each of us with something. It could be: serving, encouraging, teaching, giving, leading, governing, being merciful to those in need, feeding the hungry, clothing the naked, or giving water to the thirsty. Jesus said in John 4:35 that the fields are ripe for harvest right now. There is so much opportunity to make a difference in someone's life today. You should not feel that you have been passed by for an opportunity to do something in your life. Ask God to show you what opportunities He has opened for you. Don't be afraid to ask God to move on your behalf. And then take them because these opportunities lead into my next point.

P is for purpose. God does love you and has a plan for your life. How wonderful it is to know life has purpose.

my life *Before I was a Christian I would sometimes cry out in despair, "Is this all there is to life? Be born, strive for 70 or so years to get "stuff and then die? There has got to be more to life than this!" Just before my 22nd birthday I discovered there was. I discovered that I was not an accident to Him. He really did know me. For the first time in my life I had some kind of hope that life made sense.*

God is very aware of you and has plans for you also. Jeremiah 29:11 clearly states this. It says, "For I know the plans I have for you. Plans to prosper you and not to harm you, plans to give you a hope and a future." This is God's promise to you when you put your hope in Him. So no matter where you have been in life God promises "...that in all things [He] works for the good of those who love him, who have been called according to his purpose" (Romans 8:28).

These first three letters, H-O-P are all promises for a fuller life in God while you journey on this earth. The E in HOPE is the promise for an abundant life after your time on earth ends.

E is for eternity with God. All people are created with an eternal soul. The question is not whether a person *will* live forever but *where* a person will *live* forever. The Bible says that you have a choice to make. Heaven or hell. Both places exist. And both places are eternal. Jesus says that there is a final separation to eternal punishment or an eternal life with Him (Matt 25:46). Because of sin, you are separated from God. Yet because God loves you, He made a way for you to know Him now and be with Him forever in Heaven: through Jesus Christ.

my life *God used a crisis to get my attention about the reality of eternity. On the day I became a Christian I was fearful that my boyfriend was going to kill me. That was a day that seemed like my life was coming to an end. I had a spiritual awakening that if I had died that day then my name was not in the Book of Life and that I would not have entered heaven. Something struck my heart and I just knew I needed to do something about it. I needed to find a hope regarding my eternal destination.*

And so do you. But don't wait for a crisis to make that decision. Seek God today. I realize that spiritual questions require spiritual answers. What I'm sharing with you cannot be answered with logic. It is by faith you meet with God.

It is my prayer that you will consider the H.O.P.E. I know God gives. It will have the greatest impact on your life.

Talking about spiritual things can get uncomfortable. Maybe you've wondered about spiritual things already, or maybe this is the first time it has been presented to you. Either way, know that God allows you to make your choice.

Are you ready to make a decision? Below I've given you an example of a prayer similar to what I prayed to God the day I made the decision to take care of the spiritual side of myself. Are you ready to know God in a personal way?

Dear Heavenly Father,
I know that I have sinned against You and need forgiveness. I believe that Jesus is the way to You. Please forgive me for my sin

277

and become my Lord and Savior. From this day forward, please help me to live for You.
In Jesus' name,
Amen.

If you prayed this prayer, I am very excited for you! Welcome to the family of God! Your life will change for the better, yet the changes are not always easy. You will need to develop your spiritual life. Here are some suggestions on how to do that: read your Bible daily, talk to God daily through prayer, and regularly attend a Bible-believing church.

Always remember that God is the God of Hope and you can always trust that He will help you, provide you with opportunities, show you His purpose for your life, and bring you into eternity with Him. Now that is HOPE!

If you would like to know more about faith in Jesus Christ, please contact me. I will be more than happy to share my HOPE with you.

Prayer

Dear God,

I am thankful that You care so much for me. Help me to trust You with my whole life: body, soul, and spirit.

In Jesus' Name,

Amen.

Digging In

In what way might you be focusing more on gaining things on earth?

In what ways have you wondered if there is HOPE for you?

If you have never accepted Christ into your life, what is stopping you today?

In your own words, write what you've learned from this chapter.

His Words Of Hope

† "Do not let your hearts be troubled. Trust in God; trust also in me. In my Father's house are many rooms; if that were not so, would I have told you. I am going there to prepare a place for you. And if I go and prepare a place for you, I will come back and take you to be with me that you also may be where I am" (John 14:1-3).

† "Jesus said to her, 'I am the resurrection and the life. He who believes in me will live, even though he dies. And whoever lives and believes in me will never die. Do you believe this?'" (John 11:25-26).

† "For God so loved the world that he gave his one and only Son, that whoever believes in him shall not perish but have eternal life" (John 3:16).

† "If we confess our sins, he is faithful and just and will forgive us our sins and purify us from all unrighteousness" (1 John 1:9).

† "For all have sinned and fall short of the glory of God" (Romans 3:23).

† "We implore you on Christ's behalf: Be reconciled to God. God made [Jesus] who had no sin, to be sin for us, so that in him we might become the righteousness of God" (2 Corinthians 5:20b-21).

About The Author

Karen Wells holds a Master of Divinity with a major in Marriage and Family Counselling from Briercrest Biblical Seminary, which is located in Caronport, Saskatchewan. She is the founder of Karis Counselling Services, with one aspect of the counselling service devoted to helping women regain the power they've lost because of a past traumatic experience. As a globally-minded woman, Karen offers her services by telephone, Skype/webcam, and webinar. She also hosts her own weekly live call-in counselling radio show. As well, she facilitates workshops, speaks, and writes. Her recent book is entitled, *Even With My Knees Knocking I Will Follow God's Call.*

Karen and her husband, Simon, also provide marriage counselling services. You can learn more at www.walktogethermarriage.com.

Karen and Simon are the parents of two adult children, Angela and Dean. They also have two wonderful grandchildren, Kale and Paiton-Jade.

Endorsements

Christine Dupre is a professional freelance graphic designer. With a strong Christian faith and commitment to professional design, she offers over 20 years of talent and experience to meet marketing and advertising needs, both personal and business. Christine can be contacted at cedupre@msn.com.

Susan Lawrence edits, writes and speaks. She's passionate about pouring into women and loves to equip and encourage them. Susan has developed resources and coordinated trainings and networking for international ministries and denominations. For editing services, as well as her two women's Bible studies, Pure Purpose and Pure Emotion, visit www.purepurposebook.wordpress.com.

Alma Noefe provides virtual assistance support as a general/medical transcriptionist with experience in transcribing webinars, radio shows, conference calls, recorded phone calls, and interview calls (as well as doctors' clinic notes, surgical reports, and psychological evaluations). She can be contacted at aon_77@yahoo.com or Odesk.com for any transcription services.

285

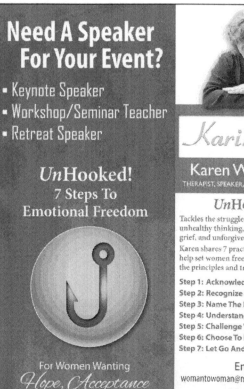

Speaking/Teaching Topics

If you are looking for a keynote speaker, a workshop speaker, or someone to teach, Karen might be the woman for your next function. She's been teaching, speaking, and developing workshops for numerous years. She has a strong passion to help women find freedom so they can live the best life possible and follow God's calling in their life.

Some topics include:

- Even With My Knees Knocking I Will Follow God's Call

- Unhooked! 7 Steps To Emotional Freedom

- Assert Without Hurt: 5 Key Strategies To Gaining Respect In Your Relationships

- Blue No More: 4 Components Of Defeating Depression

- Overtaken by the Red-Faced, Blood-Boiling Moments: 5 Ways To Master Your Anger Now

- The Heart Of The Matter: 9 Reasons We Don't Forgive And What To Do About It

- Counselling The Abortion-Vulnerable Woman

287

- Abuse Is More Than Skin Deep: 5 Ways To Escape The Unseen Pain

- Abuse Is More Than Skin Deep: How The Church Can Understand And Respond To Abuse Against Women

- Why Can't We Just Get Along?: Identifying Your Typical Relating Style

- How To Embrace A Healthy Relationship With Yourself: 21 Tips To Overcome Self-Hate

If you have another topic that you would like Karen to share at your next gathering, please contact her to see if she can meet your needs.

Contact Karen at kariscounsel@gmail.com or Skype at karenwells1.

For more information about the services and programs Karen offers through Karis Counselling Services, please go to the following:

Website: www.unhooked7stepstoemotionalfreedom.com

Website: www.mybestlifepossible.com

Website: www.evenwithmykneesknocking.com

Website: www.walktogethermarriage.com

Blog: www.mybestlifepossible.com/blog

Radio Show:
www.blogtalkradio.com/kariscounsellingservices

Email: womantowoman@mybestlifepossible.com or kariscounsel@gmail.com

Skype: karenwells1

Office: 250-624-9535

Twitter: kariscounsel

Facebook:

www.facebook.com/kariscounsellingservices

www.facebook.com/unhooked7stepstoemotionalfreedom

www.facebook.com/EvenWithMyKneesKnocking

To order copies of Unhooked! 7 Steps To Emotional Freedom

CreateSpace eStore: www.createspace.com/3687163

Amazon.com:
www.amazon.com/gp/product/1466320788

To order copies of Even With My Knees Knocking I Will Follow God's Call

CreateSpace eStore: www.createspace.com/3588185

Amazon.com:
www.amazon.com/gp/product/146108668X

ENCOURAGEMENT YOU NEED TO OVERCOME YOUR FEARS

Even With My
Knees Knocking
I Will Follow God's Call

Karen Wells

Made in the USA
Charleston, SC
06 March 2013